The Drama Teacher's Survival Guide

The Drama Teacher's Survival Guide

Matthew Nichols

methuen | drama

LONDON • NEW YORK • OXFORD • NEW DELHI • SYDNEY

METHUEN DRAMA
Bloomsbury Publishing Plc
50 Bedford Square, London, WC1B 3DP, UK
1385 Broadway, New York, NY 10018, USA
29 Earlsfort Terrace, Dublin 2, Ireland

BLOOMSBURY, METHUEN DRAMA and the Methuen Drama logo
are trademarks of Bloomsbury Publishing Plc

First published in Great Britain 2021

Cover design by Charlotte Daniels
Cover image © Boris Zhitkov / Getty Images

ISBN: HB: 978-1-3500-9268-6
          PB: 978-1-3500-9267-9
         ePDF: 978-1-3500-9271-6
         eBook: 978-1-3500-9269-3

Typeset by Integra Software Services Pvt. Ltd.
Printed and bound in Great Britain

To find out more about our authors and books visit www.bloomsbury.com
and sign up for our newsletters.

*This book is dedicated to Isabel and Roger,
my favourite teachers.
And to Jonathan, who survived.*

Contents

Preface: An anecdote

Gather round the metaphorical fire, if you will, and I'll pass on a story which has been passed down from drama teacher to drama teacher, through the ages. If it helps to visualize, all of these drama teachers are dressed in layers of scarves, much like Stevie Nicks.

Actually, this is an anecdote which I was given to ponder over nearly twenty years ago, when I was about to study for my PGCE in Secondary Drama. It's an anecdote which has often bounced back to me in a vacant moment, and is one that is worth reasoning through every now and again. At the very least, it gives an indication as to how the idea of drama teaching in schools sits within the broader framework of education.

In 1988, the Conservative government introduced the Education Reform Act, and part of this was the first statutory National Curriculum. Essentially: a prescriptive framework of every school-age child's educational entitlement, and what teachers and schools *must* cover. The notion had been put in place by Labour Prime Minister Jim Callaghan more than a decade earlier, so this wasn't merely a vogueish political tool seized on by Thatcher's ministers. Education Minister (a job which has seemingly held the same level of public popularity as Judas Iscariot) Kenneth Baker was at the forefront of this genuinely revolutionary and noble quest. Whilst the first Programmes of Study were tentatively rolled out to the teaching community in 1988 with at least one collective eyebrow quizzically raised, the legwork to put together this behemoth was done during rounds of meetings, discussions, panels and focus groups during the mid-1980s. Rumour persists that some of these discussions actually took on board the views of teachers.

Every subject was, in turn, debated. Some subjects (English, Maths, Sciences) were determined as 'core' and a vital, essential and central part of every child's compulsory schooling. With hindsight, it's perhaps strange that Computing wasn't also given its place as a core subject, as Britain stood at the dawn of a digital age which would redefine how children learned and how teachers taught. Not to matter; Information Technology (as it was labelled) found its place within the wider National Curriculum. As did History, Geography, Languages, Art, Music, Physical Education and many others. The greatest and most wide-reaching educational reform of modern-day England ... and no sign of drama. To date, drama does not feature in the National Curriculum. It never has done. Drama does not exist as a discrete subject in its own right, and it seems as though successive educational reforms, regardless of political breezes, are intent on keeping it that way. Yes, in English Literature, children will study plays and it's a requirement. Like an old sideboard, repainted over the years to keep with the trends of the day, further reforms to the National Curriculum have seen drama given the odd nod in a paragraph here, a sentence there, but fundamentally: drama doesn't exist. Why? Here comes the anecdote.

Apparently, in those crucial discussions which would redefine the entire modern educational landscape, eventually it became the turn of drama to be placed under the metaphorical spotlight. Centre stage. Jazz hands. Well, yes, went one school of thought. Drama *must* have a place in the new National Curriculum; how could it not? Shakespeare! The greatest writer of any age; his plays and poems are the beating heart of our national consciousness. We have an entire heritage industry built around our theatre history, our plays and playwrights, our world-class actors and the actor training that has developed here. Children *must*, the school of thought went, have access to drama as a subject in its own right as part of the National Curriculum. Exit stage left, pursued by a barely audible round of applause.

On the other hand, the opposing school of thought went, we need to be careful. Drama is essentially countercultural; it encourages challenges to authority and tradition. Drama will teach children how to be radical, to question, and to not unquestioningly accept what they are told. English Literature could, surely, the school of thought went, cover Shakespeare and our great dramatic heritage. But by including drama in the new National Curriculum, it would be paving the way for generations of children to be taught how to be rebellious, how to demand accountability from their elders, and potentially unleashing rivers of social unrest. And as for the teachers of this subject? Let's not even go there.

The debate was, I have been assured, keenly fought by both sides, each desperate to make their case and to ensure that drama was properly scrutinized as a subject. No other subject was held up to this level of scrutiny and debate. This has always puzzled me. Why, for example, wasn't Music debated in such a way? Nevertheless, an agreement could not be reached, so it came down to a vote. An actual 'yes or no' vote. Whether future generations of children would have access to drama as a discrete subject or not was whittled down to a binary choice because some Thatcherite ministers and political know-it-alls were cautious or sceptical about where the inclusion of the subject might lead.

You know the punchline. You know how the vote went. The ministers arguing for drama's inclusion on the inaugural National Curriculum lost – by *one* vote. That's how close it was. And that is why drama has not and does not play a part in our National

Curriculum. My own views on this have changed over the years; mild outrage and mumbling about 'political injustice' in my early twenties have simmered to a much more relaxed position where I am – ultimately – pleased that drama doesn't play a part in the National Curriculum. I relish the flexibility it brings and embrace the challenges that come with that. I love the freedom it affords me and the opportunities to devise a curriculum which suits the needs of my students.

Hang on. Design a curriculum? That sounds like an awful lot of extra work, especially compared with other subjects. And this 'freedom' it affords you? Isn't that just spin for the fact that you have to start with a blank page every time and do an awful lot more work than your colleagues in some other subjects? I'll abstain from answering. What I will say, and what I do know, after fifteen years of teaching drama in secondary schools and sixth form colleges, is that the job is as brilliant, terrifying, exhilarating, creative, frustrating and all-encompassing at it ever was. Those meetings and debates and that vote in the mid-1980s link directly to *you* holding this book today. Those men and women, all big hair and braces, put the foundations in place for where we find ourselves today. The questions and challenges remain the same, but the landscape is seismically different. How, then, with this vast open landscape in front of you, do you survive as a drama teacher? Never mind just surviving; how might you *thrive* in the profession? How do you, dare I say it, excel and be brilliant? I hope that this book might hold some of the answers to those questions.

Introduction

Creativity in schools

Whilst it isn't just each year's crop of Oscar, BAFTA or Olivier award-winning actors who can readily answer the question, it's interesting to notice just how often professional theatre makers can and do reference their earliest acting experience, when asked. Invariably, professional actors remember: that first school play, the local youth theatre group they joined, the inspirational drama teacher who nurtured and encouraged their creativity. Actors talk about this stuff in interviews all the time; let's not, then, underestimate both the impact that drama can and does have on a child and also how vividly the memories are ingrained. Personally speaking, I can't remember what I had for dinner two nights ago, but I can recall, with pinpoint clarity, the moment that my junior school drama teacher thought that there was a part for me in the school play. Unluckily for her, I also realized that by veering from the script and winking at the audience, I could steal the limelight and detract from the main plot. I bet she rues that day.

In these formative years of education, drama is often a highlight for the youngest learners; it's fun and often not thought of as a subject in the way that maths or phonics might be. It's essentially active. You can't really get very far by being a passive participant. It requires energy and effort and commitment. It doesn't involve desks or a traditional classroom environment. For some people (children and adults alike) the empty space, the black box, the drama studio, the school hall stage is liberating. The sense of play and fun is inherent and creativity can be harnessed and realized, and that empty space is the perfect blank canvas on which to explore. To others, it's sheer terror; the lack of desks and chairs is exposing and cold and frightening and please-don't-look-at-me. Tackled properly and negotiated carefully, children learn how to play successfully in the space. 'Making up stories' becomes improvisation. 'Pretending to be other people' is a performance. It can and should be liberating. Children instinctively understand performance and how to perform for an audience. I was at my friend's house and his daughter, barely two years old, finished a small bunch of grapes, plucking each one from the stalk and eating them. When she had finished eating, she held the empty stalk to the crown of her head, walked in front of us, and announced that she had a tree growing from her head, before collapsing in a fit of giggles. She had just written her first joke, sourced her first prop, negotiated her performance space and performed her material for us. This is, surely, drama.

By the time children get to school, subjects are more explicitly defined. It is critical that every student has a right to a creative education as part of their curriculum. This should ideally involve Art and Music and Dance, but I'm not here to fight their corners. Partly because I can't draw, sing or pirouette. Creativity, though, is vital to a child's educational, psychological and emotional development; the ability to think and work creatively is an extraordinarily valuable commodity and drama teaching and drama teachers deliver this in spades.

Let's take that a step further: drama is *vital*. A few years ago, I did some research work, involving drama and children who had (for one reason or another, and it was usually pretty heartbreaking) drifted from mainstream education. This was ostensibly a project about using drama skills to try and help these students make sense of some of the things in their past. That's not a new or revolutionary idea; drama therapy has been recognized for several decades and can have genuinely transformative results, which clinicians recognize as valid. What the project sort of morphed into was helping to enable these students to find their voice, to stand up and to speak in front of other people. At first, I didn't understand. Partly due to my own ignorance. I'd never done any work like this. And to start with, these students wouldn't speak. Couldn't speak? No. They all had the capacity to speak. They would not speak.

I won't lie. It took absolutely ages, and for the longest time I wasn't sure I was getting anywhere. We carefully negotiated rules for speaking aloud, and sections of the shared space for speaking and sections for listening. We started by making sounds, collectively and with our eyes closed. Liberated by the lovely feeling of filling a space with a noise, we moved towards actual words. All of these children could speak, and slowly, we started to make progress as they each took terrifying steps towards looking other people in the eye and saying words out loud. Eventually, through gentle coaxing and constant reassurance, by establishing rules and boundaries and by making sure that this was a 'safe space' where no one would laugh at anyone for anything they'd attempted, the students started to speak. From my lofty and entirely misplaced middle-class notions of enriching these young people's lives through some (I thought) really interesting plays and drama games, I came to realize that these students simply didn't dare speak at home. Never mind me, waltzing confidently in with copies of poems and extracts from Dennis Kelly's *DNA*. These children did not dare speak, and often it was for fear of violence or recrimination. It was absolutely no wonder that they wouldn't open their mouths and communicate when it came to these sessions. Once they started to speak, we could then work on them making eye contact, speaking and addressing someone, standing up and looking at someone as they spoke to them. And without fear or shame. I came to understand the vulnerability of these people and how much trust in us and belief in themselves it took to be able to stand up and take part. Let's be honest: these are only the first fledgling steps of contribution in any sort of drama activity. The project taught me that drama is indeed vital; it gives people a voice. Literally. The right to speak and to express and to declaim. Stripped back from notions about formal assessment or examination results or theatre-going, it is a communication tool. The more creativity that can be simultaneously harnessed, the better.

Then there's the very notion of creativity itself. What is creativity? It might be helpful if we all had a common and shared definition of the word. What does it mean to be creative? We all know what it means to be creative, surely. We recognize creativity when we see it. Sure we do. We can spot it in those we teach and those we know. 'She's really creative', you might be told, about someone who has a particular way with words. Or, 'I love what he's done with them, he's so creative', you might hear about someone else who has a knack with arranging pictures on a wall. Creativity appears in all walks of life and applies to us all. We are all creative, but to what degree? I'm labouring this point because the notion of creativity is bandied around a lot, as is the word itself. Its definition, though, in any real-life context, is much harder to pin down. If we know what creativity is, even if it means having different definitions or different interpretations of the word, how do we measure it? What is the unit for measuring creativity? Spoiler: there isn't one. Creativity is fundamentally at the heart of our subject, and the application or demonstration of creative ideas is mentioned in examination specifications at all levels, and yet: there is no measure for it. I can tell you how many kilometres the

Earth is from Jupiter (it's around 629 million, seeing as you asked) and how many people have been members of the Sugababes (six in total, but never more than three at the same time), but I cannot measure how creative any of my students are.

Try to see it as liberating, rather than restrictive or bewildering. As drama teachers we have to spot creativity in our students and know how to nurture it. We have to use creativity in our approaches to our classroom practice. And we have to find creative ideas and solutions to the work in front of us. Your creativity might be slightly different from my creativity, but I like to think of it as seeing a situation where someone has 'turned the lights on'. That moment where a spark happened, someone applied some logic, thought laterally, used some emotional intelligence. I'd struggle a bit with the notion that it's where 'magic happens'. Creativity isn't that. We are all of us creative, not sorcerers, and must learn how to recognize our strengths in using our own creativity as well as helping to spot it and nurture it in those in our charge. It's at the very epicentre of our subject, and whilst it's really hard to define and impossible to accurately 'measure', it needs to be the spark of the ignition of what we do as drama teachers.

Free from the shackles of adult inhibitions and social conditioning, children can be immensely creative. The genuine creativity and joy in play that can be seen in very young children tends to dissipate and get a bit lost as they get older. Older children are less and less likely to take risks. As teachers, in the British school system, locked into an assessment-overloaded curriculum, we increasingly teach to the test. And guess what? We ourselves are less likely to take risks. Therefore, in theory, it's possible that the older and 'wiser' we get, and the more experienced we are as drama teachers, the fewer risks we take. In so doing, we are closing off potential possibilities of genuine creativity. We might become stale. And we shouldn't be stale. Our students deserve brilliant drama teachers, not stale and stuck ones. If we want our students to be creative, and that involves taking risks, then we are going to have to be willing to take risks and be creative too. By engendering creativity in our students, we can establish, enable and nurture creative urges and impulses that can last a lifetime.

A subject in permanent self-defence

At the time of writing, drama is on the decline. What does that mean? It means that, in basic terms, with every year that is passing, fewer and fewer students are opting to study the subject to any level of formal qualification (BTEC, GCSE, A level). It means that fewer schools are offering the subject, and that it's becoming the preserve of well-funded and selective independent and grammar schools. It means that the subject is being pushed out of options choices at GCSE, and that lower down the school, at Key Stage 3, it's falling off the agenda or – worst-case scenario but far from uncommon – some schools are doing away with it altogether. Despite all of the brilliant and unique things that our subject can bring to a young person, and to a school community, it's on the decline. Massive educational reforms in the last decade, driven by Ofqual and pushed through by a Minister of State for Education (you know who) who was obsessed with the notion of 'rigour' and his own crackpot ideological whims, have seen our subject be pushed into the margins or drop off the grid altogether. Let's be honest: this isn't good. Not at all. The fact is that if you're reading this and you're a drama teacher, the fight still goes on and that's a *very good thing*.

It wasn't always thus, and not so long ago either. I left school at the end of the last century/millennium (just typing that makes me feel a little bit queasy). I was born into Margaret Thatcher's Britain and had spent my entire childhood and teenage years being educated by policies set out by the Conservative governments of their day. That National Curriculum? Fully up and running by the time I started junior school. My teachers, some of whom were then nearing retirement and, having been standing at the blackboard since the 1960s, were having absolutely none of it and just did their own thing. (One slightly batty junior school teacher taught us our times tables but called it 'ticker-tickering'. Obviously.) I left school within a week of Tony Blair's landslide New Labour victory and went about getting my A levels, taking a gap year (working as a waiter in a cocktail bar, travelling in South-east Asia and trying and failing to learn *Redemption Song* on the guitar) and going off to university. In the meantime, Blair's government, swept to power on a mantra of 'Education, education, education', set about broad educational reforms, which included the pioneering Building Schools for the Future (BSF) programme. This recognized that some schools had been built to serve children and communities in the 1960s, or even earlier, and were woefully out of date. Not just in lacking a fancy reception area with comfortable chairs, but in being able to meet the needs of a curriculum which was being renewed to keep pace with the then burgeoning digital era. Money was promised, and that money was poured into the BSF; a huge investment into hundreds of thousands of lives and into making real and tangible changes to the educational model. When I took my first terrified and tentative steps back into the classroom as an unqualified teacher, in 2004, it was easy to see how these changes and reforms had come to impact on school communities and those who studied and worked in them.

My own secondary school had been a 1960s relic; all rubbish glazing, leaky roofs and about three photocopiers to the entire building. The school in which I found myself 'teaching' (I was unqualified, untested and woefully unprepared back then) was flash, modern, purpose-built. Another old 1960s relic has been bulldozed to make way for this new BSF project which was complete with dance studios (with sprung floors!), a proper theatre space (with retractable seating!) and music recording studios and software (with the power to connect to the Internet!) to rival professionals. Education, education, education indeed. The school that I had landed in was in a seriously deprived area, about to be plunged into special measures, but built with serious optimism about the possibilities of drama and the other performing arts. The school had, in fact, been designated as a specialist performing arts college, thank you very much. I can remember that when I'd got my qualified teacher status and was applying for jobs, things looked different from my own 1960s relic school. I applied for a job at a school which was boasting a music studio that had been opened by the Bee Gees and a drama studio performance space that Tony and Cherie Blair had opened. How about that, eh?

I realize now that, of course, it's cyclical and that these things ebb and flow. That whoosh of money and faith and investment into the bricks and mortar of New Labour's British schools also coincided with a renewed global focus in TV talent shows. A generation of schoolchildren watched and learned. Whilst the shows in question might be somewhat dubious in the claims they made, these primetime Saturday night shows depicted graft and training. Singers, dancers, actors, performers all rehearsing and rehearsing over and over again to try and 'make it'. A bit like *Fame* meets *Opportunity Knocks*, it was absolutely no coincidence that these TV shows, selling dreams of fame and stardust to the nation, and a renewed governmental commitment to proper and purpose-built facilities came about at the same time. When I started my first (qualified) teaching job in a sixth form college in 2005, the entire Performing Arts department had around sixty students on roll. When I left that job just less than four years later there were over 500 students in the same department. This was part of a national picture, and this was the boom time, to clumsily borrow an economics metaphor. How, then, did we go so quickly from boom to (not quite but nearly) bust, as a subject, and why is this the case?

Educational reforms will always be on the horizon and Michael Gove-like figures will always be lurking in the shadows, ready to try and ruin it for a few generations of students, without ever having taught a day in their lives. Our subject remains in permanent 'self-defence'. Why? Partly it's due to that lack of status afforded by not being included in the National Curriculum. The liberation and creativity that the lack of inclusion gives us, as subject teachers, can mean that we are permanently having to fight our corner and plead our case for inclusion. I've yet to work in an establishment where colleagues haven't (good-naturedly or otherwise) trotted out the same-old, same-old jokes about the subject. I've had to try to convince sceptical or dubious parents that the subject is brilliant and worthy of their child's precious option choice at GCSE or A level and that it can be transformative and that it's accepted by all universities and … no, wait! Come back! So, if the subject can sometimes be threatened by punishing educational whims, reforms and policymakers keen to make a name for themselves, and can also be eyed with amusement or suspicion by parents and our own esteemed colleagues, what chance does it stand?

It stands absolutely every chance providing that we, its practitioners, are willing to stand up and argue its case and defend its inclusion on the school timetable at every possible opportunity. We must learn how to fight for our subject. There isn't a headteacher in the country that's going to go on record and say that they don't see the point in drama or that they think it's 'not a proper subject'. That's because headteachers are clever, kind and honest to a tee. All of them. Every single one. Actually, come to think of it, there may be just a handful out there who *say* that they love the subject – and realize that photos of a big school production can really jazz up the school website and help to sell the place to prospective parents – who don't *really* love it, and might not fund or staff it properly. There might even be a couple of headteachers who know that by choking the subject – starving it of money or a prominent place on the timetable, taught by brilliant and dedicated subject specialists – it can just slide off the curriculum in their school altogether, and that pesky drama studio can *finally* be converted into a new IT studio. Or science lab. Or bespoke meeting room for the senior leadership team. Grim, huh? Keep an eye out for these headteachers, won't you? Because the fact of the matter is that if you're going to survive as a drama teacher, if you're going to be brilliant, you're going to have to be actively ready and willing to defend the subject all the time. Don't like it? Tough. That's the way it is. Trust me. Please try to accept what I'm saying, come to terms with it and get on with defending the subject. You'll be less stressed and have more time for going to the theatre or reading a new play.

Be prepared, though, to fight for the subject, and be part of the fight back against the decline. The tide will turn; these things are always part of the ebb and flow. But wouldn't it be nice if the tide might start to turn sooner rather than later? That's not going to happen if we, as drama teachers, aren't prepared to make a robust defence of what we do and – more importantly – how it can enrich and transform the lives of those we teach. This might mean having to take colleagues to task and challenge them. Not so long ago, a boy I taught at GCSE who was an absolute 'drama star' was having his formal 'A level interview' by a member of the sixth form team to gain a place in the sixth form. As part of this process they looked at his reports and comments from teachers as well as his proposed A level choices. A level Drama and Theatre Studies (as it was then) was his number-one choice. The next time I saw the boy he was crestfallen and confused. The teacher had spent the majority of the interview session explaining to the boy why he *shouldn't* take the subject at A level. The teacher conducting the interview had pointed out that he was academic and bright and had real potential as an undergraduate, and that the subject *wouldn't* help him. I've heard this routine many times over the years. It's as sadly inevitable as hearing 'Come On, Eileen' at the end of a wedding disco. For those teachers who like to have a pop at our subject, this is usually their 'greatest hit'. This sixteen-year-old boy, though, at a critical junction in his education, hadn't heard this before and was genuinely confused. I had to do a lot of counter-explaining, and speaking to parents and providing evidence and statistics and case studies of other pupils who had taken the subject at A level and not gone directly to a life of poverty, unemployment and busking in tube stations to try and scrape a living together. I also took the teacher to task, in a coolly professional and polite way. I owed it to the subject. How can we expect our subject to exist side by side alongside its other academic curriculum bedfellows if we aren't prepared to demand that it is treated fairly and with respect and that our colleagues don't work against us? Fair's fair. We mustn't run down their subjects either. But if you're going to teach the subject, please do consider yourself an ambassador and ready to challenge lazy prejudices and out-of-date rubbish wherever you encounter it.

Why drama matters

It's faintly depressing that if this were a book about English, Maths or any of the sciences, there wouldn't be any need for the soapbox-ing and my repeated urges that you will – at some point in your career – have to defend your subject. That is, to justify it. To say why it matters. It shouldn't need stating, but we are where we are, and it's more useful to devote energies to what goes on in and around the classroom than complaining that the playing field isn't fair. How can it be fair? Most governments have ignored the arts in education, or simply paid it lip service, rather than meaningful investment and prominence. In actual fact, whilst the popularity of the subject has ebbed and flowed and also been at the mercy of political winds and educational trends, the practitioners of the subject have been doing a really fine job at pushing the boundaries of what the subject is and what it can do. Not merely to fit in with assessment frameworks and examination boards' ideas of the subject, but to really inspire and ignite students of the subject. Consequently, the 'infrastructure' around drama in schools has become bigger and more complex. Theatre companies and the people running arts organizations increasingly understand the need to engage with educational outreach schemes and also programme work which will appeal to students of the subject. Filling in the gaps is an entire cottage sub-industry of movement specialists, voice specialists, physical theatre companies, mime workshops, puppet-making classes … the list goes on. And yet, you will still have to explain why drama matters. No matter that the performing arts industry is worth billions annually and is also one of the few genuinely profitable industries left in this country. You're going to have to step up, take a deep breath and say why your subject matters.

Drama matters because it is fun at the same time as being rigorously academic; it is a training ground for intellectuals which relies on instinct and taking risks; it is genuinely collaborative but also allows its learners to discover what is distinctive and unique about themselves; it allows us to make sense of ourselves and who we are and our place in the world whilst also learning from ritual, history and tradition. This is why drama matters. It can change lives, inspire devotion and – without exaggeration – change the course of civilization. Without this being a competition, I cannot think of another curriculum subject which offers all this and at the same time.

Therefore, shouldn't an excellent drama education be an *entitlement* of students? Isn't it absolutely essential rather than optional? Instead of fighting for a place on a crowded curriculum to appease the Progress 8 crowd, or prop up league tables so that a senior leadership team can be accountable to their governors and local authority, shouldn't the subject be centre-forward in our schools' curriculum, alongside all of the other core subjects? All of this is before you start looking at the data and surveys which show how the transferable skills earned by graduates of drama are valued by employers. A drama education taken to the highest level of qualification provides a thorough grounding in flexibility, creative thinking, as well as the constant reskilling which is often demanded by employers.

To make the case that drama matters, that it's essential, there needs to be a squad of tireless and brilliant drama teachers proving the value of the subject through their work. This is the hard part. And this is where *you* come in. Teaching has a notoriously high dropout rate, certainly within the first three years after qualifying. After the global financial crash in 2008 and faced with unemployment, swathes of experienced industry professionals decided that their future lay in education and they set about teacher training. By 2012 most of them had left the profession. To help prove that this is a subject worth fighting for we need to know how to survive in our profession. Actually, we need to be aiming to be brilliant. That's not an Ofsted definition (obviously) but it's what we should be trying to be for our own students. Teaching drama certainly isn't without its challenges and the pressures placed on classroom teachers by bureaucracy and administration are like never before. If you're unlucky enough to be saddled with a poor or uninspiring senior management team that isn't going to help either. You need to hold on to your guiding principles and decide to continue to fight for the future of the subject.

Decide who you want to be … and who you don't want to be. My first head of department was extraordinarily challenging to work with. A self-confessed 'maverick' who didn't really play by the rules, that philosophy extended to all aspects of their teaching and running of what was an outwardly successful department. Administration, paperwork and the nuts and bolts of managing a team of teachers and running a department were completely secondary to this person's own whims, fancies and spur-of-the-moment ideas. This generated a toxic environment to work in which was no good for the well-being of teachers. I watched and learned. By being part of that department I saw how *not* to run a department and how to make your staff unhappy. This head of department inadvertently taught me all the ways that I could be a decent line manager (when the time came) and made me realize how important it was to make sure that teachers (and students; all students, not just a select handful) were listened to and properly appreciated for their skills and talents. You'll need to decide who you want to be. Learn from the colleagues who inspire you. And when you see dodgy practice (this head of department used to take food out of girls' hands in the canteen and chastise them for their curves) make a firm resolve to never repeat it in your own teaching. Think back to the teachers you had at school who remain engrained in your memory and decide where you fit in the broader picture.

This book that you're holding, then. What is it trying to do? Hopefully it will give you ideas and provide inspiration to help you to thrive as a drama teacher and constantly strive to be brilliant, the very best you can be. It's aimed at secondary teachers in British schools. There is, without a doubt, loads of brilliant work being done to engage children in our subject with drama at primary schools, but I wouldn't know where to start in terms of how to provide ideas or guidance. Furthermore, this book isn't about pedagogy or a training manual for upcoming drama teachers seeking Qualified Teacher Status (QTS).

There are fantastic books already out there focused precisely on that. Anything by Jonothan Neelands is going to be worthy of your time if you're looking for somewhere to start. I would hope that it would be obvious but this isn't a book about drama games or classroom activities to engage learners. Again: there are shelves in bookshops full of them.

This book will hopefully give you enough ideas to feel properly empowered, and to be able to navigate and negotiate the pitfalls of the profession and enjoy all of its best and most life-enhancing aspects. This book is coming from a wealth of experience but is, I hope, grounded in reality. In every teaching observation or lesson inspection I have been part of, whether it's internal and the inspector is a colleague or whether it's external and the inspector is a blank-faced stranger in the room, my teaching has always been graded as outstanding. Lovely. That's because I know how to deliver a quantifiably outstanding lesson which manages to both jump through the hoops and also tick all the boxes. I would also add that I am not an outstanding teacher, and don't believe that such a thing exists. We are human beings and have good days and bad days and cannot possibly function at the all-singing, all-dancing, all-classroom-management-ing level required by Ofsted *all* of the time. Yes, we should strive for excellence. I think our collective goal should be to be brilliant, to be always learning and provide a dynamic education in this unique and essential subject. But it's also important to remember a work–life balance and to go easy on ourselves too.

Now that we've thought about where our subject came from, let's focus on where we are going and how we might get there.

1

What is a drama teacher?

In all probability, if you're holding a copy of this book, then you yourself are a drama teacher. Or perhaps planning on training to become one. Maybe you're thinking of a complete career change and have decided that trying to get thirty teenagers to listen to you on a wet afternoon sounds just like the challenge you need. Whatever the situation, and all glib labelling aside, I can scarcely think of a better and more rewarding profession.

Whilst drama hasn't earned its place on the National Curriculum (for better, for worse, etc.) it has been an uncontroversial addition to most British kids' curriculum offerings in one form or another. The subject that we know and understand it to be now, with a broad swathe of academic research supporting it, as well as a wealth of pedagogical theory underpinning it, is (for the most part) a valued and admired addition to the curriculum. Take the clock back just over fifty years, and the picture is very different. To understand how our subject has evolved in an educational context, it's helpful to understand where we have come from. To paraphrase Jennifer Aniston in that shampoo advert: here comes the drama teaching pedagogy history part. Concentrate.

It's impossible to pinpoint precisely *when* drama started being taught as a discrete subject in schools. There are accounts of 'maverick' educators insisting that children stand up and act out sections of Shakespeare plays, rather than the accepted dry line-by-line-by-line reading of them, seated at desks and paying no attention to the iambic pentameter. At its core, this is drama teaching; a creative response to a 'problem'. The problem posed is: *how am I going to engage these bored teenagers with A Midsummer Night's Dream?*, for example. Rather than seeing the text as a document for analysis and literary scrutiny, the original maverick drama teachers found the creative solution. Stand up. Act it out. Get the play up on its feet. Remember that the play script is a blueprint for performance, and that you can learn more about the text by treating it as it was intended. This is a crude notion of what drama teaching is, and only really scratching at the surface of its possibilities. But it places the subject in an educational setting.

There are generations of British schoolchildren who will flinch at the memory of the dreaded 'Music and Movement', a waft-y, floaty and entirely wholesome opportunity for children to express themselves physically. The educational equivalent of muesli, if you like. A chance to expand young minds and enable them to think freely and use their bodies to create interesting shapes. That this was usually undertaken to the soundtrack of a vinyl record or out-of-tune piano, and that the participants were usually barefoot and in their underwear, might give the reader some understanding of the lack of fondness with which it is remembered. And whilst this isn't, of course, drama teaching (in anything like the form that we know it today), it is still a creative and unconventional approach to delivering curriculum material.

Drama in an educational setting (and not, importantly, to be confused with Theatre in Education) is, crucially, both subject *and* method. My PGCE cohort (myself included) would tie itself in metaphorical knots trying to work out, as our tutor had posited us, whether what we were training for was 'the coat' or ' the hanger'. Hint: it's both. It's the coat *and* the hanger, it's subject *and* method. It took a genuine pioneer to bring about what we know to be contemporary drama teaching.

Dorothy Heathcote was born in West Yorkshire in 1926 and was encouraged by the local mill owner to go and give acting a go, and get some proper training. In what seems like a remarkably generous move, he sponsored her to go and study acting in Bradford. Heathcote evidently had real potential as a performer but was told that she didn't quite 'look right' for her age, and it was suggested that she rethink her career focus. Heathcote retrained to be a teacher and, as part of her teaching practice, would implement drama games and activities into her classroom teaching. It is from this that Heathcote developed her own unique way of working, and it is this way of working which eventually became the norm in drama teaching. It's probably fair to say that there was a time when Heathcote and her methods were held in reverence, and that she hasn't so much fallen out of favour with contemporary drama teachers. It's perhaps that, since her passing, there are fewer exponents of her methodologies and increasingly innovative approaches to delivering our subject.

It was her introduction of 'teacher in role' and also 'mantle of the expert' (two strategies that are still widely deployed in secondary drama teaching) that really made a name for Heathcote and, accordingly, her reputation grew throughout the 1950s and 1960s. I'll be honest – 'teacher in role' terrifies me. I avoid it at all costs, and flinch when PGCE trainees I'm mentoring ask for my advice on how to implement it. The notion is simple; the teacher assumes a character and is quizzed 'in role' by their students to try and gain insight or information into a particular incident, subject or school of thought. As the teacher in this scenario, I find the whole thing exposing and feel really vulnerable. I'm saying this because I remain full of genuine admiration for the drama teachers out there who can switch into a local police officer or Mary Magdalene or Alan Turing or Katie Price at a moment's notice. Heathcote had cracked it, and by 1964 was teaching a full-time Advanced Diploma in drama teaching, and did so for a further twenty years. Her work was radical and brilliant. At times she worked with the young offenders in institutions outside of mainstream educational settings, and also with people with severe learning difficulties. Her method and approach might have slowly developed over time, but the values at the core of her work remained constant.

In the 1980s, Heathcote recognized that not all drama teachers had the confidence and skills that they might need and she developed her 'mantle of the expert' strategy. Much has been written about this innovative child-centred approach, and I don't intend to repeat it here. Again, she was ahead of her time, and it's remarkable that this enquiry-led process is focused on the student and their gaining in expertise, confidence and experience. Heathcote's work embodies the values of the subject at its best: inquisitive, probing, compassionate and potentially transformative. I was lucky enough to meet her once, when she spoke to a group of newly trained drama teachers. She was very old by this time, but pin-sharp, funny and – my favourite thing about her – carried on knitting throughout our group discussion. We were in awe of her. Reflecting now, nearly twenty years later, I am even more awestruck by the fact that she wasn't dressing up what she had done. She understood the values of brilliant drama teaching, and knew that her methods and approaches had ultimately made a strong case for drama as a subject to exist in its own right. There are other notable drama education pedagogy practitioners, but none with quite the reach and impact of Heathcote, even if this isn't always properly acknowledged. This book isn't intended in any way as a substitute for rigorous drama education pedagogy. It's intended to provoke thought, stimulate and generate ideas for how best to define, refine and deliver your own brand of drama education brilliance. But it would be remiss not to acknowledge that the reason that the subject exists today, and its core values, are because of a young woman from West Yorkshire and the generosity of the mill owner who sponsored her.

Is drama a facilitating subject?

Every year, when it gets to the autumn term, and my sixth form students are putting together their university applications, fretting over impending UCAS submissions and missing their homework deadlines, there's a question that I am asked over and over again: *is drama a facilitating subject?* This is a tricky one. 'Facilitating subjects' are the subjects most preferred by higher education institutes when it comes to applying to study on their undergraduate degree courses. Drama frequently *doesn't* appear on the lists produced by universities. This is often infuriating and leads to drama teachers having to defend the 'value' (a word which can be loaded with ugly connotations and hijacked at times) of their subject – to students and to parents.

Drama is *obviously* a facilitating subject. It offers academic rigour and develops a range of transferable skills in exactly the same way as all of the other subjects that are on any of these approved lists. Note also that these lists can mysteriously change from time to time and can vary from institute to institute; subjects come, subjects go. Trying to pin down the individuals who make these decisions is impossible. Believe me, I've tried. I have argued with admissions officers about why (for instance) A level Music is 'allowed' or classed as a facilitating subject, but A level Drama and Theatre – which is constructed in *exactly* the same way – isn't. It's a waste of time. Universities and higher education institutes can do what they want, and do. What we drama teachers need to understand, and always keep a grip on, is that our subject is essential and that we might need to argue the case for its inclusion from time to time. It is exciting and fun, and academic, and challenging and can unlock potential. This isn't just at sixth form and undergraduate level; this is at *all* levels.

Drama has the ability to enable students to play, to think, to create and to gain a better understanding of themselves and the world around them. It can facilitate a love of plays and theatre-going, and 'the business of going to the theatre', but this is an annex. A drama student has a whole raft of transferable skills, valued not just by employers but also by the big wide world. Drama students have to develop skills in working independently as well as collaboratively. They have to think about how to find creative solutions to problems and consider factors such as human vulnerability and emotional intelligence.

Not all drama students will manage all of these things, and certainly not necessarily to a high standard. That's fine. That's the nature of the beast. Different students acquire different skills and in different ways and at different times. Drama, however, has such scope and possibility as a subject that you (that's right, you, the drama teacher) are able to design and build a curriculum which is robust, inspiring and allows your students to find out how they work at their best. Drama, in my view, *does* facilitate. I'll paint a picture of how this can work, and not always in the ways that we plan.

A former of student of mine had been a natural, inherently gifted and talented as a performer, and made the transition from Key Stage 3 to GCSE and A level with ease. Furthermore, she was liked and admired by her peers, and was astonishingly versatile when it came to roles in productions in and out of school. It was no surprise at all when she went on to study drama at university. We were, as a department, delighted; that's another one on 'the list', another example of how exciting and enabling the subject can be. She sailed through university, got involved in drama clubs and societies, took shows to the Edinburgh Festival and emerged with an excellent degree. And it was at that point that she decided she didn't want anything more to do with drama whatsoever.

She'd become a bit disillusioned and burned out. Three years, as she put it to me, living in houses full of drama students made me realize I had had enough and wanted to see what else was out there. On one level, I was a bit disappointed (I'd started to think we might have been teaching the next Meryl Streep) but on the other I admired her attitude and the fact that she was taking control of her own career and future. Surely enough, she landed a graduate trainee job … in sales and marketing. I was a bit speechless. I'm not for a moment suggesting that a career in generic sales and generic marketing sounds tremendously boring or anything. Just that it didn't seem what this student, who'd written her own one-woman show about Madonna and the Virgin Mary trapped in a yoga class (maybe you had to be there for it to make sense), would be doing with her life.

She was justifiably proud of herself and impressed with the process. She had had to go through five – five! – gruelling interviews and task-based sessions to get the gig. She'd had to explain to people just why she was so passionate (about generic sales and marketing, despite having literally no experience of either, beyond handing out flyers at the Edinburgh Fringe) and work with other potential trainees on small projects to see who could come up with the most creative and imaginative solution to the imaginary client's needs. It was in that moment, as she breathlessly reeled all this off, that I realized what had happened. She had taken all of the skills that drama had taught her, right through school and higher education, and had convincingly presented herself to her potential employer as the Ready-Made Sales and Marketing Specialist. Of course, she got the job.

And, of course, she didn't last in the job. She hated it, and later told me that within a week of starting, she realized she was in the wrong game. When she handed in her notice, after less than a month, the company were sad to see her go (assuming she'd been poached by one of their high-flying competitors) but she was thrilled. In the space of a month, the job had taught her so much about what she *didn't* want and didn't want to do during the working day. She had so many options open to her. The point of all this is that she had all of these transferable skills at her disposal because of drama, the ultimate facilitating subject.

A tradition of theatre and performance

Whilst it's important, as drama teachers, that we are in control of a fundamentally skills-based and 'practical subject', it's also important to remember that the subject has its roots in theatre. And that theatre and drama are not the same thing; sure, they're sort of mutant Siamese-style twins, conjoined and coexisting, but they do different things and in different directions.

The very beginnings of what we might now think of as drama teaching in British schools undoubtedly stemmed from the study of plays. Let's face it, Shakespeare. There will have been others, sure, but it will have been the study of the Bard, as part of English lessons that will have started some teachers thinking about the plays as offering much more than being read aloud. I met an English teacher this year who told me that she (and I quote) 'didn't like plays'. At first I thought that this was deliberately perverse posturing, designed for a reaction. I pressed her for more, and she explained. The problem with plays, she said, is that they are too hard to pin down, too hard to always decide on what the author meant. Another issue, she went on, was that by the time a director and actors and designers have got their hands on it, it might not look anything like how she had imagined it in her head. She then went on to give a long-winded illustration of her point, using a production of *King Lear* as her example and I slowly drifted into autopilot mode, nodding and smiling as she went on.

I thought this was fascinating, though. An English teacher, and a good one by all accounts, not really into theatre. By the sound of it: not trusting a play. Worried that they were too open to interpretation. All of the things that make plays special and unique and brilliant she wasn't keen on. There has often been an uneasy relationship between English (usually English Literature) and Drama in schools. As the latter has gained status and credibility, some practitioners are unaware of what one subject does and how it does it differently from the other. It has long been a pet peeve of mine that, in schools where Drama and English Literature are taught, it is very rarely that it's the English department borrowing expertise from the Drama department. More often than not, it's schools making English teachers fill up space on their timetables by moonlighting and doing some drama teaching. Don't get me wrong; there are some fantastic people who manage to teach both subjects well and with distinction and flair. It's worth thinking, though, for a little bit longer about the things that the two subjects both share before they diverge and follow their own unique pathways.

It's this shared history of theatre and theatre performance which can often muddy the waters between the two subjects, but is the very thing that they have in common. I don't plan to provide an outline of just how Britain has enjoyed a long and much-envied tradition of theatre, theatre-making and theatre performance. There are whole shelves of libraries and bookshops devoted to just that, as well as … well, look around you. The creative industries in Britain are, at the time of writing, some of the most successful, continually growing and 'value-for-money' industries in the country. When Ofqual was consulting teachers, students and examination boards about the subject as part of its reform in 2014, what emerged was that, since the introduction of the National Curriculum, the theatre-making landscape had shifted dramatically.

The nod to the tradition of theatre and performance that had been given at the introduction of the National Curriculum in 1988 had flourished into a complete and complex industry. And the reform of the subject – in essence, deciding on what its cornerstones were – needed to reflect this. Theatre directors were consulted, as were all sorts of theatre makers. Producers and designers were interviewed. Companies who work via collaborative means (Complicite and Kneehigh, for example) were asked for their input. There was unanimity in recognizing that the post-compulsory education and training for theatre makers had changed seismically in the previous twenty years. Therefore, if drama education was going to change and adapt, it needed to remember its roots in a tradition of theatre and performance, but also recognize that the industry now provided jobs for specialists in, for example, puppet design, video manipulation and design, and a whole range of employment opportunities for the twenty-first-century jobs marketplace.

Drama education does now – and perhaps more so than ever – balance its mix of skills acquisition and a theatre/performance focus. Indeed, when the new GCSE and A levels in drama were being piloted by exam boards, many teachers remarked that there was a definite move towards them being a qualification in theatre ... rather than in drama. And that, at GCSE, the newly reformed subject looked much broader in scope than its predecessor as it focused on the business of theatre and theatre makers. As someone who was heavily involved in those reforms, I wouldn't contest that point of view at all. Whatever people think of drama, as it is currently being taught as part of a British curriculum, it has significantly developed and expanded to reflect the heritage and the cultural traditions associated with theatre and performance.

Beyond this, and briefly re-entertaining the notion of whether drama is 'the coat or the hanger' in the clumsy metaphor, it's worth pointing out that when drama is the hanger, the coat can be theatrical customs and traditions in other territories. Whilst this book is written from the perspective of British secondary school education, aged eleven to eighteen, it's not to say that some of the guiding principles couldn't be adopted in other territories. And whilst I am apologetic but honest about my lack of knowledge in terms of drama education internationally, I am completely signed up to the notion that we can use drama as a medium to deliver all sorts of topics. Not least, we can investigate the traditions of theatre-going and performance as they apply in other countries, cultures and traditions.

During my PGCE, I found myself in a school where I was struggling, trying to teach a cohort that were overwhelmingly non-native English speakers. Some of whom could speak virtually no English. Suddenly, my clever scheme on *The Lion, the Witch and the Wardrobe* seemed a bit daft. There were so many cultural and social differences between what I was trying to deliver and what these students' own experiences had been formed from. The carefully chosen part of the novel I had used made reference to a rocking horse. Not a single student in that group knew what a rocking horse was. It was time to have a rethink. Don't get me wrong; it's glaringly obvious that a fundamental part of these students' education was an introduction to and a development of understanding a new set of values and traditions. But there was no way that my planned session on using 'role on the wall' (thank you, Dorothy Heathcote) was going to have any meaningful impact on a group who didn't know the book, the story, and (as it turned out) had never been to the theatre.

My solution was, I thought at the time, revolutionary. It wasn't actually revolutionary at all, but I needed something to throw at the students. I had to have a good long think about what might work; what might bridge the gap and connect with these students so that the outcome still had some value? Quite simply: it was the *story* itself. Never mind the book, or the film, or the sequels. It's the story of the children's voyage into Narnia which captures the imagination and excites. Human beings are neurologically predisposed to respond to stories. It's been true since cavemen times. Together with these students, we used shadow play (or shadow puppetry) to tell the story. This ancient South-east Asian art form managed to fuse the plot of the book, introduce non-native English-speaking students to the idea of performing for an audience, and also nodded towards the possibilities of looking beyond our own inherited cultures and traditions when it comes to performance.

I mention this here because its simplicity is key. The fact that shadow play can still engage an audience is due to it being universally understood and its potential for emotional accuracy at the same time. Now, many (many!) years later, I'd be inclined to overthink this problem. I present this solution here as one that worked, and will always work. By shamelessly magpie-ing from another cultural tradition, and using its constituent parts, I was able to deliver my planned scheme of work to a group of learners with very limited command of the English language. The beauty of the tradition of shadow play is, of course, its non-dialogue-based approach. Sometimes, as a drama teacher, you're going to be faced with seemingly impossible challenges like this. Most of these challenges aren't, in fact, impossible. Sometimes it's best to go back to basics.

At the chalkface

Day in, day out, what does a drama teacher do? It's a very good question, and the answer might vary somewhat from teacher to teacher, from school to school and according to individual duties and responsibilities. There are constants, however, and it's worth remembering that the role of the drama teacher is unique.

Of course, as a teacher, you'll need to deliver lessons. Whether it's a potted version of *Macbeth* to a barely awake group of Year 8 first thing on a Monday morning, or whether it's a fidgety, chatty and restless Year 11 in a revision slot on a Friday afternoon, you're delivering. You're aiming to be consistent. To be fair, compassionate and ideally to inspire and create magic. Believe me, it's hard to feel inspirational or magical when it's lashing it down with rain and you're trying your best to win over a group of hardened Year 9 who have already decided they aren't picking your subject as one of their GCSE options next year.

You can only deliver these lessons once you've planned them. This does – I promise – get quicker as you move through your teaching career. It can still be daunting, time-consuming and not much fun at all. And this planning also requires you to be flexible, accommodating and willing to change all your plans at a moment's notice. I remember a PGCE trainee of mine who was extremely diligent and proudly showed me, at the start of their placement with me, that they had planned every lesson for the next three months. Commendable as this might be, there was no room for manoeuvre. Plans change, things happen, sports fixtures come and go, and you have to adapt and move forwards.

Beyond this, you're probably also going to have to get pretty good at demonstrating all the attributes of a theatre director. You'll have to work with (young, inexperienced, sometimes challenging) actors, you'll need to be able to edit and abridge a play to meet the needs of the group in front of you. In some cases, particularly where funding is tight, you might also find yourself as costume designer, lighting technician and administrator also. The number of hats that drama teachers have to wear is astonishing. We can't, all of us, be good at all of these things, all of the time. That's why it's important to take some time to think properly about the drama teacher that you want to be.

Your guiding principles

Before we start to really dig into the things you're going to need to do to be a brilliant drama teacher, it's worth pausing and having a think.

I have been inspired by teachers my entire life. Both of my parents are teachers, my sister is a teacher and I was lucky enough to be taught by some genuinely inspirational educators. The older I get, the more grateful I am. The very best teachers I have had managed to deliver the requirements of whatever the scheme of work or syllabus or exam specification was, and also add something extra. All of us remember our best teachers, and I would argue that it's because of their unique (or perhaps unconventional) approach that we remember them. The very best teachers add something of themselves to the mix and make the subject exciting and special. Without resorting to *Dead Poets Society*-style cliché, they engage and inspire the students in front of them by being distinctly 'them'. Think back to your best teacher, your favourite teacher, the teacher who 'got' you and allowed you to fall in love with their subject. It's a certainty that the teacher you're thinking of was bold enough to put themselves centre-forward in the mix and bring something of their own personality to bear on the material they were delivering.

It's actually pretty brave, when you stop to think about it. You can hide safe and secure behind the jargon of education, the meticulously planned schemes of work and the carefully controlled assessment points. You can navigate from first lesson to parents' evening to the summer holidays with ease, and without ever really needing to give too much of yourself on a personal level. Without making drama teaching sound too much like a religious cult or a yoga retreat, I would vouch that it's impossible to be a brilliant drama teacher unless you're willing to be a little bit brave, a smidge vulnerable, and give of yourself. By that, I mean that I absolutely endorse personality-led teaching whereby you completely and absolutely maintain all professional standards and values, but you also manage to give students enough glimpse of a real person beneath the exterior. There are teachers out there who absolutely don't share this view and think it's a bit barmy. Fine. That's their call.

But this is my book, and I'm here to try and show you the ways in which you can be a brilliant drama teacher. And one of the main ways to do that is to have the courage and self-awareness to bring your own personality and your own views and ideas into the mix. In fact, I would argue that it's essential in drama teaching, and perhaps more so than in any other subject on the timetable. Just consider. Students are given, in your lessons, creativity and freedom. The freedom to explore and create, the freedom to play, and sometimes this means that students will create and devise work which can be an 'acting out' of their own inner issues, or an exploration of really sensitive subject matter. Or both. And you have to facilitate that. You might be asked for your views on potentially thorny subjects. The best drama teachers will ensure that students see and understand that there are lots of possible answers with no categorical 'correct' one, but also be able to discuss their own views as part of the mix.

One of my most inspiring teachers asked me – when I was training to be a teacher, and getting it all wrong, and struggling with assessment and paperwork and plays and classroom management – a really brilliant question. I still ask myself this question today, nearly two decades later.

What sort of drama teacher do you want to be?

At first glance, the question might seem so basic as to not really be worth asking. But, pause, and have a think. You have a choice, and it's not a choice that you make once and then set in stone forever, but it's a matter of having some guiding principles. It's about thinking about your career, your teaching, your time spent in the classroom (or studio, or freezing Portakabin or dinner hall in the lesson after lunch whilst they're still sweeping up stray chips) and considering the privileged position you're in and the impact that you have. Therefore, again: what sort of drama teacher do you want to be?

Ofsted (or its equivalent in the independent sector) demands that we are, at the very least, satisfactory teachers. Most schools and senior leadership teams want us to be better than satisfactory. It's fair enough; students emphatically *deserve* better than satisfactory. Beyond the inspection-flavoured definition, there are countless ways of defining the sort of drama teacher that you might be. It's worth having a think and writing them down. Put that piece of paper in an envelope, stick it on the fridge, pin it to the bathroom mirror. Think about how much of yourself you're willing to give to this brilliant and essential subject to communicate all of its joy and life-changing potential to students, and decide on the core values and the guiding principles which will inform and underpin all that you do. Yes, there will be days when you want to crash your head against your desk in frustration or despair. Of course, there will be times when you want to skulk home after a testing day and go on an eBay spree. (It's worth making friends with the reception team at your school so you can get the parcels delivered there and then sneak them home one at a time.) It's a career; there will be ups and there will be downs. But if you have a set of values and principles which stay pretty consistent and define what you do, you have all the potential makings of understanding who you are, what you can give to your students and how you can thrive as you deliver this essential subject.

2

Building a drama curriculum

What sort of drama curriculum do you want to teach?
What sort of drama curriculum is going to meet the needs
of the students you're teaching?
Where do you start?

The first thing to consider is how much agency you have to make decisions in your school. Are you the person in charge of the subject and able to design its curriculum? If so, this might be more straightforward. If you're working as part of a larger team and underneath a line manager who makes these decisions, you might not necessarily be given the power or authority to make changes. Quite a lot of drama teachers work as single-person departments. Great! Complete autonomy! But also no one to sound out for ideas and bounce things off. On top of all this, you will also have to fit into whatever notions and ideas the leadership team at your school has for the subject.

Let me be blunt. Good senior leadership teams will trust you to know your subject, understand the needs of your students and have faith in your ability to design and deliver a curriculum that meets the needs of these students. These enlightened senior leadership teams (and if you have one at your school, count your blessings) will ensure that you have the support and resources that you need, but will also respect that *you* are the subject specialist and that *you* are the one delivering the lessons on a day-to-day basis. This should mean that you are given a blank canvas as a starting point, as well as the ability to make changes where necessary. However, and with depressing inevitability, not all senior leadership teams are like this.

I worked in a sixth form college where a senior manager, new to the college and being paid a not inconsiderable six-figure salary, brought about a 'great new innovation'. Do, always, regard any great new innovations from senior leadership teams with a healthy degree of scepticism and suspicion until they've been tested by the people who have to deliver them. This colleague of mine decided that, midway through the academic year, every single student in the college was going to sit two written exam papers, in exam conditions, and receive the grades on an internal 'results day' a fortnight later. The timetable and regular teaching would pause to facilitate this. I can remember him excitedly delivering news of this glorious step forward at a meeting of us middle managers. The room fell silent. Quite simply, it was an unnecessary and unwanted innovation. It added a series of pointless administrative burdens and made sure that staff were required to create exam papers which couldn't accurately measure what was being taught. I tried to point this out.

My A level Drama and Theatre Studies students didn't have a written exam in what was, then, their Year 12; the specification didn't include a written assessment in that year. So what would be the point of my creating two (*two*) written papers for them? What would they be on? I asked. Couldn't they be a bespoke practical assessment instead?, I suggested. No, I was told. I had the freedom of choice, the senior manager told me. As long as it was two written papers, sat in a week, all would be well.

I was younger and less experienced and less confident then. Relatively new to my first middle-management post, I didn't dare continue to present my case for the defence. Dutifully, I obliged, and created two utterly pointless written papers, and went through the grinding charade of marking them and giving feedback after the gloomy internal results day. A decade later, I know differently and would call out a bogus stunt like this. My point is this: when you see superfluous and pointless nonsense like this in your school, no matter who is setting it up, find a way to call it out. My students were in no way better off for having jumped through the hoops of this process. In fact, they were *worse* off; we had lost valuable time and momentum on our practical work. Thanks so much, high-salaried senior manager!

When it comes to your subject – our subject – you know best. It is a basic professional courtesy that you should be treated with respect and allowed to deliver your subject in a way that works. Drama can have its odd little quirks. I can think of no other subject that relies on collaborative working and an enormous amount of administration and preparation to enable practical assessments at GCSE and A level. With every new line manager I have had, I have had to start over again; from scratch, patiently explaining why the subject is the way it is and why the assessments need to take place in a certain way. If it seems like starting the work on building a curriculum at the end point with final assessments is something of a backwards step, then yes, it is. In my experience, it's best to start at the end and identify your final target. This might be a GCSE exam, it could be an A level. It might be a BTEC qualification, or it could be an assessment for the end of Year 8 to create a grade for a report. The principle remains the same. This is emphatically not 'teaching to the test' either. To design a robust and effective drama curriculum, it needs to be permanently focused towards its conclusion; this punctuation mark of summative assessment is crucial, and should also provide room for a student's future development. The curriculum you design needs to have a natural and logical curve of progression, building from one level of attainment to the next. At each level there should be a goal, and there should be a final goal for the levels of attainment in your school.

At Key Stage 4 and above (GCSE and after), the schemes of assessment pretty much take care of themselves, handed over by examination boards in their specifications. When it comes to vocational learning, such as a BTEC, the teacher has an even greater degree of flexibility ... though considerably more administration and paperwork.

So, let's take a step back and focus on the vital groundwork done at Key Stage 3 first. What do students need at this stage to hopefully inspire them and engage them with the subject? How can we, as a profession of brilliant drama teachers, make sure that we can deliver it successfully?

The building blocks

What are the building blocks of the subject? What does that mean? This will vary a little from establishment to establishment, though the fundamentals should remain the same. It is empowering students to be able to act, to be able to think creatively, to work collaboratively on text and devised work, and to be able to reflect on the work that they – and others – have created. Stripped back, at its core, it is providing opportunities for students to express themselves creatively and feel that they are in a safe space to do so. It's finding ways to deliver the core skills that students will need if they are to be fantastic drama students. Though, in time, the focus will extend and ripple outwards to encompass things like theatre-going, analysis, evaluation and an appreciation of play texts, fundamentally, the initial focus needs to be on the individual.

Think about your Key Stage 3 students (or, perhaps, your prospective students). At the beginning of Year 7, the students will inevitably have differing experiences of the subject from a primary lesson. This could vary from 'no experience whatsoever' to 'all-singing, all-dancing, every weekend and after school'. Of course, as is standard practice, some sort of baseline assessment is needed. You need to know who these students are and what they can do, as well as what they can't do. Students are not house bricks; one Year 7 class might differ greatly from the next Year 7 class, but a snapshot of their practical skills at this stage is essential. This might take the form of a short task based around improvisation, or it could involve some sort of imaginative reworking of an existing folk/fairy tale, poem or song. The best tasks at this level will enable students to express themselves in different 'directions' and allow you to see what's working, and what isn't. I am firmly of the belief that, at this stage, the focus for students should be on practical skills. Is there a real benefit of written homework in drama at this stage? Perhaps. I'd argue that it's best demonstrated in precise research-based tasks or asking students to find an artefact and be prepared to discuss it. The focus needs to be on what goes on in your drama studio from lesson to lesson. Small steps, working from that initial baseline assessment onwards, towards a goal.

Let's not underestimate the fear that some students might be feeling at this stage or, indeed, by being asked to stand on a stage. Drama teachers and successful students of the subject tend to love the freedom of the open space in the studio, without rows of regimented desks and chairs. (Colleagues and supply teachers who have to cover a drama lesson typically have an identically opposite response to the studio space.) For some students, though, the drama studio can be a daunting and frightening space. Teaching in a genuinely tough school at the start of my career, which was about to be plunged into special measures, I soon learned that some students shied away from speaking up or performing in front of others. This was because they might get a smack round the back of the head at home for doing the same. How to work round this? The solution isn't simple and it doesn't arrive overnight, but the use of praise as a motivating factor, as simple as that might seem, still works wonders. Watch how the unconfident child's blink rate increases when they are genuinely praised, for instance. Some students won't welcome praise in front of their peers or in anything like a public setting, so a degree of tact and discretion is paramount. Bit by bit, nudged on by your praise and the consistency of your presence and behavioural expectations, students will start to feel safer and safer in the studio space. When students *do* start to feel safe in your studio, then they might start to express themselves. With discipline and structure, students will realize that they can do well in the subject, and they will start to *want* to do well, too.

You need to make a note, a record, of the first assessment you do. How best to do this? First, you need to establish – for your own peace of mind – what it is that you need this assessment to show, to reveal. It could be that each student receives a letter or a number grade, maybe with a plus or a minus, to indicate their initial level of ability. Your school might well adopt an entirely different sort of internal assessment monitoring and tracking system. That's fine. But there is absolutely nothing stopping you from devising your own, using it in lessons and assessments, and then translating the assessment data into the school-friendly format for reporting and tracking. Make the assessment framework work for you. Don't go down the route of pointless written exam papers or rogue assessments which tick a senior leadership team (SLT) box, but don't benefit the students or help you in your delivery of the subject. Configure a system that you can use and flexibly adapt as you go. Do you share your assessment framework with your students? I would argue that, as the student progresses further and further through the school, the common understanding of the assessment framework becomes more and more important. At Year 7, the notion of assessment can sometimes be like a carrot and a stick. Pupils will want to do well and assessment itself can be used to encourage and motivate. Conversely, some students become panicked and stressed by the notion of assessment and won't perform well. In my current job, I don't tell my Year 7 students when they are being assessed. They're being assessed most of the time, in most lessons, in fact, but they aren't aware of this. By approaching assessment this way, students are more likely to perform 'naturally' and be less focused on the assessment outcome itself.

The skills that students need, then. At the most basic level, students need to learn how they can use their voice and their bodies to communicate things in performance. That's what acting is, right? We can overcomplicate it all we want to, but that's what actors do, and that's what is also at the heart of a robust drama curriculum.

Let's say, then, that the initial assessment gives each student a score from one to ten for both their application of vocal skills, and their application of physicality/movement skills. You need to create a task where a student can demonstrate both. At this stage it doesn't help to overcomplicate either aspect; there's no merit in asking students to demonstrate an accent if they can't, first, be heard when they are speaking on stage. Likewise, asking for a demonstration of a facial expression is pointless if a student isn't actually facing the audience in the first place. If you're a drama teacher who worries about how much time you spend reminding younger students to face the audience when performing, then WELCOME TO THE CLUB! Joking aside, it's a reminder of the basics and fundamentals that only become established through routine practice and repetition. A simple practical task which students can complete in pairs or small groups, and allows them to speak and move, will give you all the evidence you need to make a formative assessment judgement. Splendid.

It goes without saying that you'd want to have some sort of curriculum plan in place for the term ahead, but I'm always keen to remind PGCE trainees and younger teachers not to plan *too* far ahead. You need to get a real understanding of that group, of those students, and adapt your curriculum planning to meet their needs. Your curriculum design at this level needs to have enough built-in flexibility to allow you to subtly and gently steer each group of students to the same destination – summative assessment – but, perhaps, via slightly different means. Recently, I taught two very different Year 7 groups. Both were learning how to create their own film trailers. This is great fun; you can consolidate understanding of the theatrical (and cinematic) genre with montage, characterization, direct address and a consideration of how to work in a specific theatrical style. Once I'd delivered the heartbreaking news that each group couldn't devise a trailer for a superhero movie (or *Fifty Shades of Grey*, as one boy waggishly suggested), they set to work, and it became clear that the needs of the two groups were very different. The first group was lively, bright, focused and confident; they could produce fantastic snippets of movie dialogue and deliver them with conviction. However, they couldn't move. Not literally. But any sort of organized movement or anything requiring coordination reduced them to giggles, firstly, and then a seething mass or argument. My focus for this group then became silent movies; producing scenes from silent movies, and thus forcing their hand into working collaboratively to improve their movement skills. The focus was simply on precision and detail in using movement to communicate to an audience. By contrast, the other group could move absolutely fine, but their understanding of genre and how to distinguish between different genres was pretty weak. I was able to adapt their lessons to think about delivering the same line of dialogue in a range of different genres, and building from this to eventually telling the same story in different genres. We started by looking at words and how they might be displayed using different fonts, colours and sizes, and then moved to what 'voice' these different words might need. Both groups started at the same point, and ended at the same point, with the same assessment. I was able to 'tilt' and adapt my lesson planning so that the routes varied slightly, but the goal remained the same. In so doing, each group got a more targeted focus on the area that they most needed to improve.

In my current role, I am part of a department of five teachers, and we all adopt the same 'umbrella' project focus, but each of us will deliver the agreed curriculum in a way that plays to our strengths as teachers, and also pushes our students to improve on their weakest areas and be better all-rounders, as we get to know them better. We might, for example, look at physical theatre with Year 9. Having established that physical theatre isn't a synonym for 'fighting and screaming and throwing chairs at each other', Year 9 can enjoy the challenge of coordinating in time with music and working in rhythm and without dialogue to create meaning. I like to explore physical theatre by looking at extracts of the theatre company DV8. One of my colleagues, on the other hand, will lead their students through the Frantic Assembly school of devising. A third colleague, by contrast, won't subscribe to the notion of a specific theatre company but will focus on movement and 'coding', almost like a basic form of Laban-style notation. We each of us look at our students and try to think about what sort of learners they are. We think about the place we have to get them to, the end goal, the assessment point. And we think of the best possible way to get them there, which will play to our strengths as well as stretching and challenging them as students. This isn't 'teaching to the test'. It's adapting a curriculum in a smart way to meet the specific needs of your learners.

Playing to your individual strengths as a drama teacher is vital, especially at Key Stage 3. At GCSE and A level you will have less of a choice about what you deliver. You didn't do any classical drama as part of your own training? Well, you've still got to get your A level students through *Medea*. Best start doing some brushing up at home. At Key Stage 3, it isn't like that. You can still find ways to deliver things you aren't familiar with by using methods that are closer to your comfort zone. I recently worked with a teacher in a school who had been asked to deliver physical theatre at Key Stage 3. He was worried that he couldn't move, had no coordination and also had no training or background in that way of working. We talked, and he let slip that he was actually pretty good at fencing. That was his way in. We devised a series of lessons where he could use the patterns and rules of fencing, principally focusing on footwork, to enable students to move together with rhythm and coordination. None of us can know everything. We all have classic films we haven't seen (*Casablanca*), classic novels we haven't read (*Nineteen Eighty-Four*) and classic plays that we've neither seen nor read (*The Cherry Orchard*). I remember being honest when I filled in a subject knowledge appraisal form as part of my teacher training. I also remember my mentor being alarmed that my knowledge of shadow puppet theatre and kabuki theatre was non-existent. Fifteen years later: it's still virtually non-existent. There will be people out there who will be outstanding at work like that. Know what you're good at, have confidence in your own subject knowledge. But also have the knowledge that none of us can be leading experts on all aspects of our subject, and that's fine too.

In terms of developing your students through Key Stage 3, it's well worth spending some time thinking about progression. Your school might well have its own in-house levels of attainment, and if this is the case, these are usually aligned with National Curriculum levels. This is actually of only limited use. At the time of writing, the National Curriculum for English at Key Stage 3 makes two cursory nods at our subject. It says that in terms of 'Reading', students should read a wide range of fiction and non-fiction. 'Plays' are mentioned, with the further specification that 'Shakespeare (two plays)' is 'studied'. Note the use of the word studied, and that this falls under the subheading of 'Reading'. There is no instruction or requirement for the *practical* study of these plays. I find this infuriating; practical study of play texts is undoubtedly the best way to explore them, to fall in love with them and to understand what they mean. The beauty of a play text is that it's open to so much interpretation, particularly when staged or explored on a practical basis. Yet the stipulation here is for reading. Sigh. The other nod towards our subject comes under the subheading 'Spoken English' and mentions 'improvising, rehearsing and performing play scripts'. It doesn't say how many, or how often, and the emphasis is very much on vocal delivery. Fine. But that's short-changing the subject if the focus isn't on the total experience of realizing play texts or creating something through improvisation. There's also no coverage of self-reflection or analytical appraisal. The National Curriculum might be invaluable and the metaphorical backbone for classroom teaching in other subjects, but when it comes to drama, there are other more useful models to adopt.

The drama curriculum that you build needs to be robust, have in-built flexibility to meet your learners' needs and allow students to develop the key practical skills in the subject, through text-based and non-text-based work. You could devise your own assessment scale which falls in line with the appropriate levels as determined by the National Curriculum, and step progression logically through this scale. Consider whether it's useful to develop key practical skills in isolation and without context. Hint: it isn't. Rather than teaching 'vocal skills' in isolation, it's far more effective to embed the assessment of vocal skills alongside the assessment of physical skills. I've seen some schools' curriculum assessment maps which separate the elements of key drama skills into discrete 'topics' of their own and assess them in isolation. This can start to pull the subject in line with spoken-word and public-speaking examinations, if looking at voice in isolation, for example, and it's also fairly dry. Students will make more progress in the development of their key practical skills if they are assessed within the framework of a creative task whereby students perform a final product. In Years 7 and 8, you will have greater success by delivering short (really short in the case of Year 7) tasks with clear guidance and a performance outcome, whereby you can assess practical skills development, and students have the opportunity to create and explore. This is where the real learning takes place.

At some point in Key Stage 3, if the focus is eventually narrowing towards the preparation for GCSE (or its equivalent vocational qualification), text is going to have to be introduced. When is best to do this? Students aren't house bricks and you know your students better than I do. You should feel confident, though, in using Year 7 for practical skills development without ever picking up a play text. You can use artefacts, songs, poems, objects, articles – pretty much anything – and use practical tasks to explore and release dramatic potential. By Years 8 and 9, some text work will need to be introduced. When I joined my current school, drama had morphed on to the curriculum as a breakaway subject from the English department. What this meant was that, in reality, students didn't have any drama on their timetables in Year 7, and in Year 8 – their first formal introduction to the subject – they picked up a Shakespeare play. Admittedly an abridged version of the full text, but Shakespeare nonetheless. In small groups they would rehearse it and then perform it to an audience. Some students through sheer talent, force of effort and an astonishingly instinctive grasp of the text managed to deliver a confident and reasonably accomplished performance. Most, however, didn't. They didn't have the bedrock understanding of their own practical skills from prior study to then begin to work out how to apply said skills. As a department, we redesigned the curriculum and were allowed to introduce drama to the curriculum in Year 7. Just one lesson a week in Year 7 made an enormous difference to the finished product of these Shakespeare plays in Year 8. You cannot expect students to meaningfully engage with a play text without the foundation of practical exploration of the key drama skills.

Picking texts to excite and engage Years 8 and 9 is tricky. Particularly during that dreaded part of the academic year when Year 9 have made their GCSE options choices and those who haven't picked drama start to shut down, drift off or just plain refuse to take part. For just over two decades, the National Theatre has put their money where their metaphorical mouth is and, each year, has commissioned some of the most exciting British playwriting talents and asked them to write a short play for young performers as part of their *Connections* series. Some of these have been so successful that they have burst out of the seams of the *Connections* project and become well known in their own right. Dennis Kelly's *DNA*, for example, has become part of the canon for drama (and English) teachers in just over a decade. These plays are as good a place as any to start, and there is bound to be something which will engage and excite the students you are teaching. They are also compact in terms of length and realistic in terms of the demands that the texts make on young performers. Notes and appendices in the published editions are also really helpful for teachers considering how to approach the practical exploration and rehearsal of these plays.

There is a world of plays out there and (more on this in Chapter 5) there is often a depressing reliance on plays which are dated, stale or simply not realistic in terms of challenge for young performers. Tread cautiously also with those plays which are written specifically to fill a gap in the market. Plays which are written for young performers but are only published online or never seem to receive any public performances. These plays are often focused on a specific subject matter and can be reductive in terms of theatrical scope and don't always provide enough room for students to approach the text with real imagination. I won't lie; I've used these plays and they do – sort of – work. They will fill a gap in your lesson planning and students will work with one another to rehearse and perform them. I've found, however, that the outcomes can be very limited and often depressingly similar, usually due to the limitations in the writing. Over time, I realized that it was better to study a lengthy extract or decent abridgement of an existing play text than grabbing an 'oven-ready' play off the shelf.

At Key Stage 3, working towards GCSE and beyond, you need to map your curriculum across the three years. Start with short tasks and projects in Year 7 and gradually increase the length of these tasks along with the demand. Introduce play texts at some stage, but make sure that there has been meaningful practical exploration using the key drama skills beforehand. The beauty of the subject being freed from the shackles of the National Curriculum is that *you* get to design the topics and areas of study to suit *your* students and draw on *your* areas of specialism. See it as a positive; it genuinely is. From making sure that giggling Year 7 remember to 'face the audience' when they perform to giving Year 9 the opportunity to present an extract from a play text and receive criticism and feedback, you pick the pathways that will work for you. You might not get it right the first time. That's absolutely fine; none of us do. If you have colleagues in your subject, ask for their advice, learn from their experiences. The bottom line is that you will become a better drama teacher by becoming more confident in the subject and using your own assessment framework along the way. There might be some awkward conversations with line managers or senior management now and again. As long as you are fulfilling the needs of your school and your department in terms of assessment and reporting, you have the flexibility within the subject to make it work for you and – crucially – make it bespoke and work for your students. Aren't they the lucky ones?

The A word

Assessment. Ahhhh, assessment. That can either be said with a sigh or through a scream. It's an essential part of any sound educational pedagogy, and it's also the bane of many people's lives, as well as a useful classroom tool, an appropriate method to determine levels of achievement and, on occasion, a political football.

How so? Quite simply, without having any assessment in place, it's not possible to reliably and accurately measure what a student can or can't do, and how much progress they have or haven't made. Great. Job done. Only, it isn't. There's formative assessment, which you can deploy to make an initial judgement about a student's skills or level of ability. There's also summative assessment, where you subsequently measure what a student can do at the end of a task or process. Perhaps more usefully for us, as drama teachers, we are asking: what can the student do now that they couldn't do before? Progress is expected and some myopic educational policymakers and senior management teams in schools might try to insist that progress is made at a specific rate, or in a certain way, or in a particular order. Resist this as much as possible. Drama doesn't always work like that. The nature of creative and practical exploration in a studio setting might mean that different students move in slightly different directions, and acquire skills at different rates. That's fine. Don't be bullied or coerced into being told that *all* of your students must be able to do X before they move on to Y.

Assessment is also one of the eternal political footballs, at least within English educational policymaking. News articles and radio bulletins will refer to studies or research projects which suggest that students are tested too often, and in meaningless ways so that the assessment findings themselves are bogus. English schoolchildren are tested more than their counterparts in any other nation in the Western world. There would be an easily argued defence for this if it were also the case that our educational achievements were amongst the best in the Western world. They aren't. Each newly appointed Secretary of State for Education will want to make their mark with bold policies and flashy initiatives. These often involve the notion of more testing, even more testing and then some further assessment (testing), just for good measure. When Michael Gove was Secretary of State for Education (a period that many surviving classroom teachers remember with a cold shudder or wincing grimace), he certainly made his mark, reforming the curriculum at all levels and pushing for more (this was the buzzword) *rigour*. I'm still not sure what that means. How is rigour measured? What's your rigour and is it the same as mine? What rigour seemed to mean in this period was an increase in testing and assessment. A GCSE qualification in Drama with one exam board, for example, had not involved any sort of formal written examination; following the wide-sweeping reforms in 2014, the same exam board had to include a written exam which accounted for 40 per cent of the qualification. There seemed to be an in-built understanding that written examination (at desks, in an exam hall) somehow had more *rigour* than an assessment of practical skills as demonstrated in performance. I refute this idea completely. A practical assessment can – and should – demonstrate a different type of achievement and understanding than a written assessment; each is pointing in a slightly different direction. Yet it has crept into lots of educational thinking that a written assessment is somehow more useful, or more accurate, or *better*, than its practical counterpart. Make sure that you design appropriate assessments which are fit for purpose; some should be written, some should be practical. The method of assessment is crucial; ensure that when you are plotting assessment points through your curriculum design that each assessment is going to be able to accurately capture the information that you need.

When I was training to be a teacher, assessment was the big buzzword. It was drilled into us throughout our training. Every lesson had to have some form of assessment somewhere in it. Beyond that, the assessments had to be appropriate for different student 'learning styles' (something else which seems to have slipped from the education agenda, having had its day in the sun) and needed to be rigidly plotted into lesson and wider curriculum planning. In theory this is a nice idea. What this school of thought doesn't allow for is the learning and discovery and experience that can happen over long-form practical exploration. When it comes to improvisation and devising original work, this can take absolutely ages. Without the structure and framework of an existing script, students have to simultaneously work out what they are going to say and do as well as how this saying and doing might happen on stage. Initial ideas might well run to nothing, and people can hit brick walls and explore a multitude of 'dead ends' (all of this is a normal and healthy part of the devising process) before ending up on the trajectory to the performance of the final piece. It would be difficult to make any sort of formal assessment of this process, one which is so stop-start and forwards-backwards, certainly in its initial phases. However, it mustn't be disregarded because assessment can't easily take place. The experience and the genuine learning that can take place during this sort of process are invaluable. Creativity doesn't always fit neatly into boxes and is impossible to measure. It's only through practice and experience, though, that students can learn how to be creative and how to harness and apply their own creative skills.

It's worth considering two types of assessment – practical and written. When planning your curriculum and what you're going to teach, you'll also need to design marking criteria so you can capture and record students' achievements. These can be as simple or as complex as you need them to be. You might consider marrying the command words of the different bands/levels on your mark scheme so that they marry up with those of the exam board(s) you use at GCSE and A level. These could be as simple as: unsatisfactory, limited, satisfactory, good, outstanding. Those five words, for example, could be mapped across any numeric or letter grading scale and could be used to inform feedback and assessment reporting. At all levels. Getting students used to the assessment models you use is important, too. So many teachers don't routinely share the assessment framework and criteria that they are using with their own students. I struggle to understand the reasoning behind this. If we go to pass our driving test, we need to know what to do (and, crucially, what not to do) if we are going to be successful. We'd struggle if we just got in the car and the assessor asked us to drive to a destination. Make sure that your students know what you are looking for when you're assessing them, and *how* you're going to measure them. If this seems strikingly obvious, good. That's how it should be, though lots of teachers don't adopt this method. It might be, then, that the wording and structure of other existing assessment frameworks in place at your school could be a starting point for you to structure your own purpose-built assessment framework.

When drama was reformed as a subject in 2014, Ofqual set about a wide consultative process with teachers, theatre makers and such. The result of this process (it took absolutely ages; I seem to remember doing work for the reform alongside three consecutive years' Christmas trees) was the Subject Content. This is, if you like, the holy grail and the information and wording that all of the exam boards had to use to then structure their reformed qualifications at GCSE and A level. Within this document (again, freely and publicly available) are the descriptors for what a student of the subject would need to do to achieve a level two, five or eight in the subject at GCSE (or the alphabetic equivalent at A level). So, you might want to adopt these level suggestions from GCSE into your planning for assessment at Key Stage 3. There isn't only one successful route to designing assessment, and it might take some trial and error until you find a wholly successful method which works for you, but there are starting points out there if you're stuck.

You can easily and accurately assess students' practical work, both in rehearsal and in performance. Using whichever grading/level or alpha-numeric system you've chosen to use, you can make a value judgement about what it is that you're seeing. As the educational world has become increasingly obsessed with the notion of tracking and data monitoring, make sure you always record this assessment score. Somewhere. Anywhere. It's quite normal for Key Stage 3 students to have more practical work than written work, so evidencing this practical work is important. In rehearsal, you'd expect students to be focused, on task and engaging with the practical work you've set. Whether it's working from a text or improvisation/devising, the work is most likely to be collaborative. You could assess their cooperation, their willingness to collaborate, their creative contribution or the skills that they demonstrate throughout the preparatory process. In performance, you'd be looking for a demonstration of practical skills which are in line with your assessment brief. Perhaps something more polished or final, but this can be captured and graded in exactly the same way.

Depending on the resources available to you, an easy and accurate way to capture evidence of performance work is to record the final performance itself. This can be played back to students so they can see how their own work communicates to an audience. This can also be stored as evidence for any work scrutiny or inspection that you might find yourself plunged into. Sometimes, the mere presence of a camera can actually make more gullible students up their game. I fondly remember (and when I say fondly, I mean 'with absolute horror') a Year 9 class who I always taught after lunch on a Friday. Pumped up on chips, football and the promise of a weekend ahead, they were permanently excitable and frequently difficult to get to focus. The video camera was my secret weapon. One lesson it was still in the corner on a tripod having been used by a colleague in the lesson before lunch. The presence of the camera brought about an unusual quiet and focus in the room. 'Sir, are you recording us? Is this an assessment?' Of course it's an assessment, I told them. I need to record your rehearsal as evidence for your report, I lied. Why isn't the red light on the camera? Well spotted, the LED is broken, I improvised. Where a Year 7 class might be inclined to seize up and not perform to the best of their ability at the mention of the 'A' word, for older students, the thought of the session being recorded and forming part of their grading and reporting can encourage focus and discipline. Try it; it even works with an old, broken camcorder.

Then there is written assessment. There is absolutely no reason why the level/band descriptors that you've chosen to use for the practical work can't be mapped across and used for the levels and bands for written work. Consistency and familiarity with these command words will help students to understand the context of their assessment and how they might best make further progress. Written work is – of course – a straightforward way of capturing and recording assessment data. Whether this is stored in exercise books or electronically, it can demonstrate evidence of learning at a glance. The problem here is that, for the overwhelming majority of drama students, there is genuine disparity between the standard of the practical work and their written work. Essentially, they are generally better at practical work than they are at putting pen to paper/finger to keyboard. This means that if you only have evidence of written work as your assessment data, and your students fit in with this national trend, your data is skewed and not telling the true story. I would advocate only occasional written tasks in Year 8 (possibly) and Year 9. Having a mixture of reliable assessment data which covers practical *and* written work is the most robust and secure way of ensuring that you can track your students' progress throughout Key Stage 3 from beginning to end.

Written tasks should take the transferable command words from your relevant GCSE (or equivalent) specification and embed them lower down the school curriculum. Typically, students are going to need to develop skills in description, explanation, analysis and evaluation. By the time they reach GCSE, exam boards expect students to be able to demonstrate all of these skills at the same time in a ninety-minute (or thereabouts) examination window. At Key Stage 3, it is best to split up the appropriate command words and try to assess them in isolation on simple written tasks. You might, for example, ask a Year 8 student to describe the acting skills demonstrated by a classmate or professional performer. By Year 9, you could ask students to describe the acting skills demonstrated, and also evaluate how successful the actor was. Students will be developing these literacy skills in other subjects and using them routinely, but writing about drama appears to be something that even bright and capable students struggle with. Whereas the practical skills tend to be demonstrated from instinct and through mimetic observation and experience, writing about those same skills can baffle students. If you can drive a car, you learned through practical experience and became better at driving by being on the road. I'd argue that giving a written account of the practical movements and skills you demonstrated during a car journey where you were the driver would be trickier. When students find it harder to write about practical skills, we shouldn't be surprised. Look at any of the main exam boards' grade boundaries, at any level, and see how there is a significant difference between achievement in practical and written assessment. Therefore, we should buy into this and make sure that our assessment judgements lower down the school follow this pattern and pave the way for GCSE.

When it comes to assessment, start at the end. Whether that's the end of the academic year, the end of term, the end of the project or the end of the lesson. Ask yourself: where do I need the students to be by the end of this? And work backwards from there. How much assessment is needed … without it being overkill? You can make sure that your assessments keep a regular and reliable check on your students' progress, accurately measure what you need them to and also fit into any school or departmental-wide assessment strategy. To do this: look at your students and work out how you might change or adapt existing projects or assessment strategies to meet their learning style or their needs. I'm always curious when I see teachers in online forums asking for specific suggestions and advice from other drama teachers as to what they might deliver with their own students. I always think: I don't know your students, so how would I know what's going to work with them? (There's a second-tier argument which goes: how do you know that the advice you're getting from other teachers is any good?) My curriculum topics and artefacts and texts can vary from group to group and from year to year. But, by the end of each year, my students are ready to move to the next stage of their education or take some sort of public examination or assessment. I couldn't tell you *what* to teach your students, but there are ideas here on how to structure an effective curriculum, what that curriculum needs to cover and how you might assess students' progress and record this evidence.

A final thought on assessment. Don't do it for the sake of it. Over-assessment is utterly pointless and a waste of your valuable time. It's as futile as having *no* assessment at all. I mention this because, whilst I can't conceive of a situation where a teacher wouldn't implement any assessment whatsoever, I'm all too aware of schools where over-assessment is the norm. Barely a few weeks of term seem to have passed and teachers are being asked to stop their curriculum delivery and make a formal assessment of what has been learned. This can be a nonsense. Call it out when you see it. In a nice way, obviously.

Assessment at examination

Having designed a robust assessment map for Key Stage 3 and ensured that it moves logically and incrementally through levels, it should ultimately prepare your students for further study of the subject at Key Stage 4 – GCSE or level 2, as it might be called, depending on the type of assessment. By this, I mean that students are equipped with an understanding of, and an ability to demonstrate, the key practical skills within the subject and also have experience of creating original work as well as scripted text. Any qualifications at Key Stage 4 will need students to develop on these skills and push them further, ready for a more gruelling assessment. Gruelling? Sorry. Rigorous. I'll be focusing mainly on GCSE and A level, as they dominate the 'market' in qualifications here, but other qualifications (BTEC, IGCSE, etc.) are available.

It's no exaggeration to say that the reforms in the subject in 2014 were seismic. Exam board specifications had previously come and gone, but these reforms – which is where we are now, at the time of writing – moved the subject into previously unchartered territory. At GCSE, gone was the emphasis on small projects, process drama and the optionality of written exams. In came set texts, long written exams and – guess what – more assessment. Students were going to be assessed more and have to demonstrate a wider range of skills and gain an understanding of an even broader set of skills which many thought turned the GCSE (its title is 'GCSE Drama') into something resembling the old 'Drama and Theatre Studies' at A level. This wasn't an accident. Ofqual, under the direction of its fearless and idealistic leader, Michael Gove, had a fixed eye on the future *employability* of students and how this might affect international league tables, competing with STEM subjects and the ruthless exam-passing factories of the Far East. This meant that theatre makers of all backgrounds were brought in to consult on the shape and format of these new qualifications with an input on theatrical design and, at A level, the role of the theatre director and the influence of theatrical practitioners. The skills set gets broader; students are required to demonstrate an understanding of practical design skills, even if they don't physically undertake design work themselves. Conversely, students can opt for a practical design skill as their specialism and be assessed on their work in this area (costume design, set design, etc.), but still have to demonstrate an understanding of acting skills, their own and others.

Low-level panic set in amongst the drama teaching community. Teachers fretted about how they were going to move to this new structure of assessment and cope with the shift in emphasis from practical to written work, whilst also preserving their sanity. Simultaneously, it took all of the exam boards much longer than had been hoped or anticipated to have their specifications successfully accredited by a scrupulous and forensic Ofqual submission process. Working for one of the boards as I did at the time, I remember the drafting and redrafting of mark schemes, assessment models and passages of instructions. The hope being, of course, that at the end of this process there's a specification that not only achieves the official Ofqual stamp of approval but teachers might be excited about teaching and students might find engaging and stimulating. This was a very tall order. Teachers were, it's fair to say, dismayed by the percentage of the qualification which could be achieved through practical work (typically the practical performance of both devised and scripted pieces) versus the amount which was achieved via writing, be it coursework or a formal written examination. Panels of teachers were consulted by the exam boards and Ofqual, but the subject content was fixed and is as it remains today. Each current GCSE Drama qualification must constitute a written exam which makes up 'no less than 40 per cent' of the qualification. Furthermore there was a cap, in effect, on the amount of the overall qualification which could be achieved through practical work. Set texts were a feature, as was the devising (whereas previously it had been an option) and watching of live theatre, which caused something of a headache. And so, it proved very hard to please so many people. I remember attending a conference of theatre makers which was well attended by representatives from a large number of arts organizations and companies. Representatives from an internationally renowned theatre company were exasperated and took the exam boards to task for their approach to devising, which was seen by the company as reductive and in no way representative of how they or other working theatre companies devised original work. Of course, it was going to be a tall order to keep everyone happy, but the remit from Ofqual was so strict and left so little room for manoeuvre that it created a set of GCSE qualifications from four exam boards which looked very similar. For what it's worth, of course it wasn't going to be possible or in any way realistic to expect fifteen- and sixteen-year-olds to create original devised work in the way that an internationally renowned theatre company might do. Structure and guidance would be needed, as would some sort of written account of the process. Throughout this reform process – which lasted over two years, from first meetings about curriculum reform to initial delivery of the new specifications – I was still working as a teacher, and continued to worry about how these new qualifications were going to impact my colleagues and my students.

These qualifications are designed as two-year linear qualifications, but I am well aware that a significant number of schools deliver them over three years instead, starting in Year 9. If this is the case for you, then your curriculum design and mapping will necessarily differ from a proposed three-year map across Key Stage 3, as discussed here. What should remain the same is that whatever the exam board you follow is asking you to get your students to deliver at GCSE is the starting point, and your planning at Key Stage 3 segues into this.

Live theatre became a real headache too. As part of these new GCSE qualifications, students had to analyse and evaluate the work of others. This meant seeing some theatre in performance; students' understanding of what they have seen is then assessed in their written exam. This opened up a previously unexplored minefield. The National Theatre (I promise I'm not employed by them) had broken the mould and launched its genuinely groundbreaking NT Live service in 2009. This meant streaming high-quality live theatre into cinemas globally. The inaugural performance of *Phèdre*, starring a transfixing Helen Mirren and brilliantly directed by Nicholas Hytner, was a great success (Michael Billington, reviewing it in the *Guardian*, gave the performance a full five stars, whereas when he had reviewed it 'live on stage' he gave it four stars) and effectively legitimized the recording and streaming of live theatre. The floodgates opened. Not only the National Theatre but other subsidized arts organizations, West End producers, opera and ballet all jumped aboard this lucrative gravy train. High-quality, high-definition productions captured with well-rehearsed and nimbly choreographed camerawork could now be enjoyed in arts centres, church halls and community venues the length and breadth of the country and beyond. I've seen some NT Live productions which I genuinely can't distinguish in my own memory from others that I've seen 'live on stage' in terms of experience and quality. The problem came when exam boards had to decide which route to adopt in terms of students watching these 'live' performances.

It's worth being aware of this because you will need to build into your curriculum planning some sort of live theatrical experience; you have to create the opportunity for students to watch 'genuinely live' theatre and, at the time of writing, declare this officially via the exam boards for Ofqual purposes. Some exam boards won't allow students to write about a theatrical performance which isn't 'genuinely live'; that is to say, that the students weren't in the same room as the performers at the time the performance happened. Other boards are more flexible and will allow students to write about a streamed/ digital 'live performance' provided that students have also been to see some 'genuinely live' theatre. The first and most immediate argument here is one of accessibility. If you live within the M25 or easy reach of London, then you and your students will have year-round access to a range of genuinely world-class theatre productions, with frequently generous discounts for school groups. Should you not live within easy reach of the capital, the picture looks very different. Therefore, the argument goes, streamed 'live performances' are democratic and it will mean that your students – wherever they may be – can experience a piece of (hopefully) high-quality theatre for the price of about two cinema tickets, and pretty close to home. This arrangement solves a lot of problems for teachers, students and schools – often strapped for cash and wary of releasing pupils from regular timetabled lessons to go to the theatre; digital 'live theatre' is a fantastic compromise, though not all exam boards saw it that way. Even in exceptional circumstances, where a student may be absent or subject to illness, there are some DVD recordings of high-quality 'live theatre' which could be deployed. The fundamental and unanswerable question is whether a 'genuinely live' local amateur dramatics performance of an Agatha Christie thriller, for example, is a *better* experience for students (who need to be able to write in enormous detail about acting and design skills seen in performance, let's not forget) than, say, a streamed production of *Billy Elliot: The Musical* which isn't 'genuinely live'. Without wishing to be demeaning to amateur dramatics groups (I saw an amateur production of David Mamet's *Glengarry Glen Ross* which, frankly, knocked spots off its most recent West End revival), I'd be opting for the recorded performance of the one about the boy from the mining community who wants to be a ballet dancer. Every time. It's surely about the quality of the performance itself rather than whether it's streamed or not. There is absolutely no substitute for the genuinely live theatrical experience, but if this proved too costly or too unavailable or too impossible for some students, then a streamed performance can still deliver the goods in terms of examination requirements. Glad we got that sorted. Except, it wasn't sorted.

This broad church adopting of digital theatre wasn't an approach which was warmly adopted by some prominent members of the theatrical community, unfortunately. Once the industry newspaper *The Stage* got wind that some exam boards were willing to allow students to write about digital theatre screenings, it was petrol on a bonfire. A coterie of established and much-loved household names – Zoe Wanamaker, Brian Cox, David Harewood, Sheila Hancock,

Meera Syal and many others – wrote an angry letter to the *Sunday Times* denouncing these new rules. It rolled on. The industry network group National Drama piled on, also signing the letter. Whilst I absolutely agree with these actors' views about the inimitability of the live theatrical experience, our thespian community failed to understand the challenges and realities faced by students and teachers in schools today. You will need to think about this and work within your school's set of rules to enable students to see *something* that they can write about. For a number of students, digital theatre screenings will prove to be – on balance – the best overall option available. It's also really important to get this part right. Writing about live theatre is something that students struggle with, certainly initially. As teachers and subject specialists, we have had years of practice, so we are able to critique different aspects of what we are watching as well as following the plot, and laughing and clapping in all the right places. Students, even bright ones, need to learn how to do this over time. It is very much an acquired skill. Then comes issues of practicality. How many times can you take students out of school to see something? How can you make sure that what you're going to see won't be rubbish and will give students plenty of opportunity to write about it successfully? The research you do here is critical. Let me remind you of a little-paraded fact but a fact nonetheless: you are paid to work for a fixed number of hours per week and a fixed number of days per year. There should be no expectation that teachers should have to schedule theatre visits – which are a stipulated *requirement* of the GSCE curriculum – outside of working hours. I'm not trying to suggest a rigid work-to-rule culture, but there is an argument that students *have* to be given time out of regular school to attend a matinee theatre performance. Whatever theatre you're planning on taking students to, make the case for it, even if it means that they miss regular lessons. This isn't a 'jolly' or a theatre trip for entertainment's sake. It's a vital part of an academic qualification, and you know your students best and what theatre is likely to make them sit up and take notice. I would argue that taking GCSE students to see one 'genuinely live' theatre performance during the two years of their course is fulfilling Ofqual's requirement, but is the bare minimum in terms of the students' experience and understanding of theatre as an art form. If you're struggling or spoilt for choice (lucky you!), then have a look at reviews or see which companies or organizations might produce supporting materials, work packs or workshops to accompany the production you are going to watch. These are often really useful in terms of contextual study, and are typically well written, too. It's even worth looking online to see if a theatre has staged a recent production of the play you're going to see and whether they created a work pack for teachers which might still be available.

What is certain is that you're going to have to prepare your students to write about the theatre that they see. The task differs only slightly between exam boards and all of them are asking students to provide an analytical and evaluative account of what they have seen. A response could focus on acting or theatrical design skills. Therefore it's important to teach all of the different aspects of the production seen so that students have flexibility over the question that they choose to answer and have a full and detailed understanding of live theatre. It's also an Ofqual requirement that students study the play as a whole, as it will constitute one of the texts studied as part of the course. There are two pathways which can help students succeed in their writing about live theatre.

Firstly, give them as much practice as possible and make use of online resources to facilitate this. No, you can't take Year 10 out of the classroom every other week to go and see a bit of a locally staged production so that they can then write about it. But you can certainly make use of a wealth of online resources which use high-quality recordings of live productions, either in part or in full. The National Theatre (yes, them again) has recently made a large number of their filmed productions, originally captured for the purposes of NT Live streaming, available to teachers and students in schools. This is a treasure trove of resources. It's also free, and you can dip in and show your students scenes or moments from a production. This is where I would start in Year 10 (or before, if you think your students are up to it). Start with a small scene or section and ask students to discuss what they've seen. Sharpen up their vocabulary when it comes to description; what they're describing should have the sort of clarity which means that the person reading it can picture the performance in action. You can replay the clip as many times as you need. Once students have become more confident at describing what they are seeing, move them on to the higher-order skill of analysis. This is the bit that students tend to find the most challenging when it comes to live theatre. Keeping notes of what they've seen and what they (and others) thought or said will sharpen up students' analytical skills and be a record of what analysis looks like. Finally, get students to evaluate what they are seeing, and this means constantly working on developing an evaluative vocabulary which goes beyond 'good', 'alright' or the sort of shrug and a grunt which probably means they are generally indifferent. Students are experts in their own lives at describing and analysing and evaluating and it is worth reminding them of this. They will excitedly and animatedly describe the plot of a film or what happened at a party last weekend. Similarly, they are experts at reading your – and others' – body language; they know what a frosty silence and an icy stare means. And fifteen- and sixteen-year-olds aren't renowned for being shy and unwilling to be vocal about their opinions. They are *highly* opinionated, as a rule, and willing to tell you what they think about something, all the time.

The skill that needs developing and finessing here is the vocabulary and justification to support the evaluation. Don't underestimate that this is a skill which takes time to develop and students will struggle with. Persevere with them. Gradually increase the length and complexity of the clips, eventually building to a full evaluation of acting and design skills as seen in a full live performance.

Secondly, develop and display in your studio (we'll look at studios and resources more in Chapter 3, so bear with me if you're consigned to a draughty mobile classroom which lets the rain in and doesn't really constitute a studio space) the vocabulary that you want students to use and become familiar with. Make sure that this vocabulary becomes a natural part and parcel of their own practical work in class. When you are asking students to stage scenes and when they are performing extracts in class, or they are presenting moments of their devised drama as part of the development process, use the same sort of vocabulary that you'd expect them to use in their work on live theatre. Make description, analysis and evaluation a familiar and unfrightening part of the students' GCSE course. Get students to keep a record of these lessons. My own students can scarcely remember what they did an hour ago. I know that if I try to get them to remember and write about something they did last term, I'll have no chance if they didn't make some sort of notes at the time. I've also given up trying to dissuade those who make notes on their phone. If it works for them, and they engage with the process, that's the most important part. Don't fight it.

The other significant part of any written exam is going to be responses to the study of a set text. These texts are always in something of a state of flux with different boards adding and removing texts occasionally. There is a wealth of supporting material available, but often at a cost. Some of it is great; well written, properly edited and will support your students and help them in their understanding of the set text in terms of theatrical potential. Sadly, there is also material out there which is sloppy and not necessarily clearly focused on the assessment objectives of the qualifications at this level. The temptation might be to rely on existing support material at this stage, but nothing – absolutely nothing – is any sort of substitute for detailed practical exploration of the text, solid note-making and repeated practice of questions in a format as close to exam conditions as possible. You will know how your students learn best. I used to create lots of jazzy handouts and animated PowerPoint presentations before I realized that my own students didn't engage with these as well as when I made them make notes from either me talking or a group discussion where we shared ideas. I think this is true of lots of GCSE students; handouts can easily be left on classroom floors, in the bottom of school bags or shoved in a folder, never to be seen again. When students have a stake in their own learning, and this even applies to note-taking, they are more inclined to listen and to engage with what's going on. This also saves you hours of work which often goes unread and unloved.

By A level, we would hope for better. By that stage, students should be being pushed towards the sort of independent learning that would be expected of them in higher education. Too often, students will expect to be spoon-fed and want to see model or exemplar answers. These are only useful to a point, especially if students are then labouring under the misguided idea that they simply need to recreate what they are reading in a slightly different format. By the time a student is in sixth form, the building blocks and key performance skills should have been acquired and properly consolidated. This means that as the qualification becomes more demanding, and requires understanding of a broader range of more complex texts, as well as theatrical practitioners, the student can harness the skills that they have developed through their Key Stage 3 and GCSE learning to be successful at A level.

As part of the subject's reform, a distinction was made between two different types of assessment. Written examinations, those which are sat in examination rooms under nationally agreed conditions, are classed as 'examination assessment'. Sure; no argument with that. However, the practical exams, where students perform to an internal assessor or a visiting examiner, aren't classified in the same way and are labelled NEA: non-examination assessment. The same goes for any coursework. Basically anything that falls outside of the traditional exam format is classified as NEA. There will be transferable and interchangeable skills between the two and it's a sanity-preserving device to start to work out how you can make links between the different qualification components so that students can learn more effectively and you can feel less like you're fighting a losing battle.

Finally, as part of their course – whether at GCSE or A level – you'll need to prepare your students for practical exams. If you're working on a vocational qualification, you'll be doing this throughout the course in any case. And, as a special treat, you'll be designing the assessments and marking them too. Vocational qualifications have been significantly reformed in the past decade. When I started my teaching career, they were very popular. In my first week in my first teaching post, the headteacher of a school explained to me why he thought they were such great qualifications – 'They're a licence to print grades', he said. I was gobsmacked. What he actually meant was that students could take and retake (and retake, ad infinitum) their practical assessments until they achieved the highest grade possible. As teachers of vocational qualifications, we were strongly encouraged (much like in the way that muggers strongly encourage their victims to hand over their money) to do just that. The level of scrutiny and external checking of the qualification was very scant indeed, certainly compared to how it is now. At the time of writing, there are *much* stricter guidelines in place about how evidence is captured, how assessments are graded and how often they are taken, and how feedback is given. Rigour has certainly become more prominent in the world of vocational qualifications and, in comparison to a couple of decades ago, this can't be a bad thing. If vocational qualifications don't necessarily carry with them the same kudos or cachet as their more traditional academic counterparts, that's fine. Vocational qualifications best suit a certain type of student and there is a real virtue in the flexibility of these modular qualifications and how they can be coordinated and delivered. But if we are going to tell students that they are somehow *equivalent* to GCSEs or A levels in some way, then the qualification needs to be as robust and willing to withstand external scrutiny and verification.

As part of a GCSE or A level, practical work is where most students excel. Have a look at any of the exam boards' marks or grade distribution curve graphs for the practical components of their qualifications, and then compare them to their written component counterparts. Where the written assessment results follow a typical 'bell curve' model, the practical skills tend to look like a snow drift, with more students at the higher end of the mark range. Why is this the case? There's an argument that the subject is optional at the examination stage and is going to attract people who are interested in it. Sure, but the practical components of other comparable subjects don't see the same sort of outcomes. It's because this is the part of the qualification which (most) students love and is why they've picked it. They get to play, to explore, to create, to step out of themselves and see the world in another way. None of those things should be sniffed at, and practical work seen by students at GCSE and A level can be inspiring and memorable. Not always, of course, but in my years of schlepping across the country as an examiner of practical work, I can still remember individuals, and devised work, and set designs and costumes that exhibited a level of talent and skill which can only come from genuine passion and an engagement with the subject under the guidance of a talented teacher. Not for a moment do I think that every student who has picked drama as one of their options is brilliant and committed and able to produce amazing work. Students at this stage are often making choices in their practical work which are based on instinct as well as trial and error. Certainly, a lack of emotional maturity or access to formal acting training, due to their age, must mean that the best practical work comes from a talent which has also been nurtured and refined and developed through a focused rehearsal process. I'll never forget, from my time as an examiner, the GCSE student who was the last to make an entrance in the pretty average exam performance of a somewhat under-rehearsed comedy. This girl had natural charisma, poise and the sort of comic timing you'd expect from someone three times her age. She had all the qualities of a young Julie Walters and was not only significantly better than all of her peers but also working at a level way beyond the top end of the mark scheme. I remember her as I also remember, watching A level devised pieces, an ambitious reworking of the story of the sex workers who were murdered by a serial killer in Ipswich in 2006. This student-created piece used documentary and verbatim techniques and successfully referenced DV8 as a practitioner. These talented students produced a visceral piece of work which left the audience – me included – in stunned silence when it finished. Before we retreated to the teacher's office to discuss marks, I had to ask for a moment outside and try and compose myself, having been genuinely moved by watching sixth form students reclaim a series of tragic events to give a voice to women who had been murdered.

What did these pieces have in common? The same that all successful practical work does. A teacher who had chosen wisely, whether it was an extract of a script with judicious casting and neat opportunities for the performers involved, or the sort of subject matter and practitioner which could inspire students in their thinking and demonstrate an exciting connection with one another, as demonstrated in performance. The best practical work is presented by students who have teachers who know them well and have helped match them to material where they can flourish. I always feel faintly depressed when I see teachers who use the same texts or the same scenes or the same extracts year after year, regardless of the students they have in their cohort. Success with a particular play or extract one year does not guarantee success the following year. The original success was an alignment of material and its suitability for *those particular students*. Resist the temptation to return to the same text or extract or devising subject matter because you got great results with it two years ago. Those students have moved on and the ones that you have in front of you now are different. They deserve our wisdom and experience and our commitment to treating them as individuals.

3

Creating, performing, responding

'They're fine in my lessons.'

Here's a plea. Don't be the teacher that says this sort of thing. It happens in schools, from time to time, and it's often in meetings or discussions about more problematic students. Where there might typically be a consensus about the issues that a particular student is creating, a voice of lone dissent saying, 'They're fine in my lessons,' doesn't help matters or endear us to our colleagues. If you're lucky enough to be the sole teacher who delivers the one subject that will, despite all other issues, continue to engage and motivate a difficult learner, be thankful. I've been on both ends of this scenario. Knowing that you are delivering the one subject that is still making a meaningful connection with a disaffected student is fantastic, but it can also bring with it feelings of even greater responsibility. Being on the other end of this is even worse; you feel that you can't engage this wayward pupil and that you're a rubbish teacher, and your colleague isn't helping matters by making you feel this way.

The reason to point this out is that all of our students learn in different ways. This isn't about an outdated notion of prescribed and rigid learning styles. Some students will naturally engage with the brilliance and creative opportunities that our subject affords them. Others will feel daunted and intimidated by practical work, or the notion that there are rarely definitively 'correct answers'. Some students might simply shut down, or rebel and resist. The learning environment will also come into play here. Where the open studio space fills some students with excitement and joy, it will prove to be an arena of terror and exposure for others. For students who have largely switched off from school and continue to show little interest in their subjects, there will still be a few who will find that the drama studio, for example, or football pitch or other non-traditional teaching space might still capture their interest. As drama teachers, we need to be aware of this; it can be one of the reasons that the student might be 'fine in your lessons', but not elsewhere. The relative amount of empty space and lack of desks and classroom equipment in a drama studio (or, indeed, football pitch) can somehow strike a chord with students who are, elsewhere, disruptive or disengaged. Whilst any teachers need to be adept at negotiating the needs of our students, simultaneously and in one space, as drama teachers we also need to be considerate of the learning environment and how this is managed. Our subject, at its best, can be used to connect with the most disaffected of learners.

I remember being asked, a number of years ago, to come and see if a drama lesson might help engage a particularly problematic group of students. There were seven students in this Year 8 class, some of whom had support workers. Their educational needs were all different, but what they had in common was a previous refusal to engage with traditional schooling, and a real inability to focus on any meaningful tasks in their lessons. From the outside, it looked as though these students didn't *want* to make progress. Whilst they weren't rowdy (they were far too low energy for that, frankly) or violent or aggressive, they often couldn't sit still. As their teacher would start talking, they would often just walk away from their desk and go and stand and stare out of the window. They might just put their head down on the desk in the middle of a task and feign sleep or actually nod off. Different teachers with experience of teaching challenging students in unconventional settings had come and gone, and lots of different subjects and approaches had been adopted. Success still proved elusive.

When I was approached, it wasn't because I was any sort of specialist in terms of working with students outside of mainstream education; I was simply asked to come and see if, by delivering a drama lesson, these students might be able to be engaged. The first time I saw them, I watched a genuinely fantastic teacher trying, floundering and eventually failing to engage them. It was a little bit heartbreaking to watch. At the same time, I started to look at the different students (only seven of them) and see if I could see what they might have in common. Essentially: what might be the way in? I asked the teacher this at the end of the lesson. We drew a blank; it didn't seem as though they had anything in common, other than proving too challenging to be educated in the mainstream. I asked the teacher if there was anything they particularly liked. She sighed. 'Horror films', she suggested. 'They all love horror films.' I did a bit of digging. Whilst there is an entirely separate argument about Year 8 pupils existing on a cinematic diet of hauntings, possession, decapitation and graphic gore, I was willing to try pretty much anything to see if a connection might be made. The other thing that had caught my eye in the lesson was one student who, every time they passed a display noticeboard on the wall, would hit it. A quick punch. Not too forceful, not too aggressive, but it caught my attention. After the lesson, when it was just me and the teacher in the space, I noticed that the display noticeboards around the room were covered in photos and eye-catching displays of other students;

school trips, productions, sports team glories, that sort of thing. The disaffected Year 8 that I had seen were being surrounded by success stories whichever way they turned.

If a series of specialist teachers and support workers hadn't been able to engage these students, what chance did I have? It wasn't my input, of course, which unlocked the door. It was the use of drama as a medium for delivery as well as a rethinking of the learning environment which managed to make an impact. With only the notion of horror films to guide me, I devised a series of lessons which could be used to deliver some key literacy skills and might just help these Year 8 students to sit down and focus. I created a bespoke missing person newspaper story, and formatted it so that it looked like it had come from a real newspaper; it looked, to all intents and purposes, like a genuine artefact. The trick, of course, was that the language used in this newspaper was at a level that was appropriate and accessible for these particular students, and the article was constructed in such a way that it read more like an airport paperback thriller than a piece of genuine journalism. Beyond this, I created bespoke props. A ripped and dirtied teddy bear, several 'found diary entries' suggesting that the missing person might have had their suspicions that they were being watched. Then, the pièce de résistance: an audio recording, 'captured from a local police surveillance facility' (I had to deliver that with a straight face), which appeared to have captured a woman talking on her mobile phone on her way home, as approaching footsteps grew louder and louder. Hokey? Yes. Clichéd? Absolutely. But with enough recognizable tropes and hallmarks from the opening scenes of horror films, it was quite easy to use these artefacts together to help allude to some sort of grisly goings-on.

I also reorganized the chairs and desks in the space so that the environment looked and felt different as soon as the students walked in. With all of the wall displays newly covered in large sheets of white paper, each with the newspaper article on them, I had also briefly muted the goading images of the successes of others on the walls. The students' piqued interest was visible the second they walked into the space. Here was a bespoke and entirely different learning space. Crucially, it didn't actually resemble any sort of learning space they might have encountered. We were now working as a team in a police station, determined to solve this strange case. If you're struggling to picture this, imagine the *Crimewatch UK* television studios, but on a much lower budget and with fewer gadgets. The students sat and listened as their regular teacher gravely informed them that she needed their help. Ordinarily, she explained, she wouldn't ask them to get involved in this sort of thing, but she just had this hunch that they might be able to help. They were hooked. We went a step further. The teacher I was working with was a non-subject specialist so we agreed that we would deploy some 'teacher in role' work and I would be introduced as a taxi driver who had given a lift to the missing person just before their disappearance. I don't really use 'teacher in role' in my own lessons. Mainly because I'm not very good at it, as I've previously mentioned. I deployed it as a strategy quite a lot during my teacher training, where I started to understand its value as a process drama tool, but I've never really fancied myself as much of an actor or thought that I'd be able to keep a straight face for long enough, so I've steered clear. I bit the bullet with this Year 8 class, though, and my colleague – who was admirably game – played along brilliantly. Don't get me wrong, these changes to the learning environment and medium of delivery didn't play out like some sort of present-day miracle. These students, prone to disaffection and fidgeting, weren't transformed instantly into some sort of *Midwich Cuckoo* clutch of upright, focused and still learners. What was entirely different, though, was that learning was able to take place and it *did* take place. For the students' regular teacher, this was a relief and revelatory. An observer might have argued that this wasn't a drama lesson. That would be missing the point. This was a lesson which engaged *really* challenging students and delivered part of their literacy strategy. Its success lay in its use of drama techniques to do this. What it taught me was that adjustments to the learning environment can be crucial. Let's be realistic here; you can only do so much to change the learning environment. It wouldn't be practical to change this for every lesson. But these students who were – frankly – *not* fine in anyone's lessons had demonstrated that there was a way to get through to them. As you move through your teaching career, you might never encounter a group as challenging as this. What is still worth considering, of course, is where and how students learn.

Our subject, by its very nature, is ideally suited to kinaesthetic learners; those who learn best by doing, by taking part and through experience. Whilst our subject is an academic pursuit, an ancient practical art form is at its core, and practical work is at its heart. Whether it is the student's own practical work, or the study of text created for performance, or the demonstration of others' practical work in a performance space, it is a subject with feet and in motion. Drama is at its best, its most vibrant and most essential when it is actually *alive* in the teaching space.

Fundamentally, our students need to be given opportunities to create work and taught how to do this. They need to then be given a forum to perform that work; a forum which is safe and enables them. Finally, they need to be taught how to respond to this work, be it their own or the work of others. This is a cyclical model which fits any practical art form and can be taught from early years through to university level. These are the central tenets of drama teaching. Before looking at them in further detail, however, it's worth considering where you're going to be teaching and what you're going to be teaching with.

The teaching space

Throughout the book thus far I've mentioned the words classroom and studio and this needs some distinction and clarification. These two things are not synonymous or interchangeable. Some people reading this might read the word studio and want to throw this book across the room. Studio? Studio?! Some people are forced to deliver drama in far from ideal settings and the notion of a studio might be beyond their wildest dreams. I'll come to that in a minute. I have taught and seen drama being taught in purpose-built drama studios, dance studios, classrooms with rows of desks, school halls, school cafeterias, empty stages, theatres, playing fields and even the corridor outside the senior management team's office. This was an occasion when a fierce and fiery colleague of mine, sick of senior management taking over her teaching spaces when she was due to teach timetabled lessons, decided to 'give them a taste of their own medicine', as she put it, and taught a noisy practical session in the main thoroughfare of the school. To this day, there's part of me that salutes her principles and willingness to take a stand. There's another part of me that thinks there might be better ways to negotiate than this, especially with the people who direct your duties and responsibilities in the workplace. Still, the point stands that the spaces that we deliver our subject in are many, varied and potentially taken from us for other pursuits.

A word of caution is needed here. I have been to, and know of, a great number of job interviews where the school in question has acknowledged its relatively poor or inadequate drama teaching spaces and gone on to provide an assurance that plans are afoot to transform existing spaces or build new ones. Sadly, I've seen a number of these proposed transformation projects either meet the proverbial cutting room floor or be kicked into the metaphorical long grass. In order to recruit decent drama teachers, some schools will promise the earth and might not necessarily deliver on those promises. I know of one recently advertised Head of Department teaching position which provided lots of detail about the forthcoming investment in new teaching spaces and facilities. On the day of the interviews, the shortlisted candidates were all told that the plans for this renovation were being shelved. This stunt has happened at too many different job interviews for it to be coincidence, surely. Why is this perceived to be acceptable? It isn't acceptable at all. If a school has chosen to have drama as part of its curriculum, then it should make sure that its teaching spaces (and resources) are appropriate. We wouldn't expect our colleagues in science to deliver practical laboratory work in a desk-lined classroom, and nor should they. It would be laughable if our counterparts in PE were told to teach football or hockey in a classroom. That last suggestion might attract derision. It is no more or less laughable than the expectation that a drama teacher might successfully deliver their subject in a classroom space. Or, rather, a space which isn't fit for purpose. And yet, alas, this happens all the time. In one respect, things are better after two decades of overhauling school buildings and facilities. There aren't as many of those old 1960s comprehensive school relic buildings left, and most purpose-built modern sites have specific provision for drama teaching. Which is as it should be. When it comes to being brilliant drama teachers, at whatever level we are working, it is a basic requirement that we should be able to deliver our subject in a space which can meet students' needs in the curriculum. You might have to do some patient explaining or present your case as to why you can't teach that devising lesson with a lighting and costume candidate as they all work in the style of Frantic Assembly at the back of the hall as the remnants of lunch are swept up around you. Whatever it is, hold your nerve. Food and Nutrition couldn't be delivered without a space which replicated domestic cooking equipment. A swimming teacher would be sunk without a pool to instruct in. Make sure that you and your students are able to meet the demands of their curriculum in a space which works.

What is an ideal drama teaching space, then? There isn't an oven-ready solution, but there are factors which are a constant and worth considering. In an ideal world, you will have a multifunctional studio space and a separate classroom teaching space *or* a single space which cunningly includes elements of both of these. From my own experience, I've never managed to find that truly successful space which manages to double as both practical studio and classroom. I've either ended up with a studio and an adjacent cupboard full of exam tables and chairs, or I've had a classroom with a bit of a space at the back of it. Neither of which is wholly appropriate. In one of my former jobs, I was lucky enough to be part of the team which was overseeing the design of new teaching spaces in a brand new building. At a planning meeting, the architect unrolled the fancy paper and pointed out all the spaces, which included a purpose-built drama studio and another for dance. On the paper, in the corner of the drama studio, was a large square box with an 'X' in it, taking up most of the room. I was puzzled and asked what it was. The architect told me that he'd assumed we would want a piano in the space and maybe some other musical instruments. After a lengthy pause I explained why that wouldn't necessarily be of much help. What this did mean was that I could try and bid for most of the things that students and staff would need.

A drama studio space is sometimes referred to as a 'black box'. In an ideal world – and let's dream big here, shall we? – you want a large room which either is painted black or can achieve blackout through curtains and blinds. So that you can show how theatrical lighting works, of course. So, whilst we're at it, let's get some of that in, too. There should be enough space to accommodate your class sizes when they are broken up into smaller working groups to complete practical tasks. Your drama studio should also double as a small performance space, which can be used to stage scenes or extracts in lesson or host examination performances or smaller studio productions. Some proper sound equipment to go with your lighting equipment would also be really helpful; that way, students can learn about theatre design but also deploy these elements in the scenes they stage and in the work that they create. Of course, there is an issue of cost here. It's a potentially expensive outlay or investment for a school to make. As drama teachers we have to stand our ground and recognize that students are only likely to excel in the subject if the facilities they are taught in are appropriate. At a recent training event, a drama teacher told me that she was proud that the fundraising car washing day that her sixth form drama group had organized had brought in enough money for her to buy some second-hand lighting equipment for her studio. Without wishing to knock either her ingenuity or the formidable commitment that her students had demonstrated, I become a little bit sad when I hear stories like this. Is drama not worth investing in? Don't schools recognize its potential, not just for those who study it but for the school community as a whole? If you reposition that anecdote slightly, and it were an English teacher who had raised the money so that her class could have a set of books to study one of their set texts, you'd have every reason to be alarmed. It would be an indictment of the underfunding of our education system where strapped-for-cash schools can't make ends meet. So often, though, it's the case that drama teachers have to use school productions or sideline fundraising tactics to keep their subject afloat. Our subject deserves better than this. We, as professionals, deserve better treatment than this. And, most importantly, our students deserve a learning environment which is *at the very least* fit for purpose. Stand your ground and state your case politely.

There comes a point towards the end of my academic year when my studio space starts to become a bit problematic. For those of you reading who might be inclined to play the world's smallest violin for my 'plight' here at having a studio – I know. Having taught in cupboards and classrooms and on fields and in leaking portable accommodation, I fully acknowledge that having a fully functioning drama studio isn't something that all subject teachers are able to enjoy. My studio becomes problematic, particularly for my GCSE and A level classes, when we have completed all the practical exploration and assessment work of the courses, and now need to consolidate all of our study of set texts, practitioners and live theatre into something that resembles working revision notes and exam practice. I have tried – and failed – to do this successfully in a studio space. I have used jazzy PowerPoint presentations, digital resources and special chairs with a built-in writing table, but to not much avail. This goes back to the discussion about the learning environments that we create and how they enable learning and give students an appropriate space to learn in. Just as the drama studio space is ideally suited for practical work and practical assessments, it doesn't help students tune in to the written tasks that they face. Why? They walk into your studio, a place which for several years has been different, has been 'other' and something of a sanctuary from the desks-and-chairs environment of their other lessons. The studio space has represented the opportunity to play, to create, to learn by doing and by watching and feeding back. It might not be possible in your school, but if there is any way you can relocate your groups to a classroom for their written exam preparation, it is something that I would strongly encourage. I have seen amazing teachers who are able to transform their multipurpose space into practical studio at one end and mini-classroom with a whiteboard at the other, and somehow finding room for their desk in the middle. I have also seen teachers use lighting in their studio to create 'zones' for different tasks. The repetition, predictability and familiarity of these tactics help us put students in the right mindset to carry out written work. That's not to say that by moving a rowdy and rebellious group of drama students to a classroom they will transform through some sort of sorcery or magic into a model class of children, eager to crack on with their written exam question practice.

Ultimately, don't underestimate how much the learning environment and surroundings have to do with how students learn, and what they will be more inclined to engage with. Some of this will be out of your control; every school is different and you are given the hand that you are dealt. Don't be afraid, though, to state your case – politely and firmly. You know what sort of space and what sort of facilities you need to deliver the subject, and we must resist any senior management shrugging or vague excuses as to why the students of our subject can't have parity with their peers in any other subject and be taught in an appropriate learning environment. It must be an essential requirement.

Stuff to teach with

This can be something of a minefield. It is the case that our subject isn't always cheap and that it requires regular investment to keep it buoyant and afloat. It is also unavoidably the case, though, that you will need stuff to teach with. That's not unreasonable, though sometimes drama teachers might be made to feel as though they are being unreasonable by asking for essential equipment. You will need resources to support your delivery of the subject and to enable the students' learning. What stuff do you need? Where do you get it from? And are there teachers of any other subject who can be found in their kitchens late on a school night fashioning a papier mâché model of a dinosaur for an upcoming project, or creating quizzes with chocolate prizes to test students' knowledge of Brecht?

You will, of course, have a budget. Or rather, your *department* will have a budget. Whatever that budgeted amount is, you'll always be able to argue that you could do with a bit more. I'd suggest looking at your curriculum planning, taking all years and levels of attainment into account, and thinking about your needs and wants. What are the things that without which you wouldn't be able to deliver those lessons? Beyond this, what are the things you'd like, which would make the delivery either easier or more enjoyable? Make a list of both of these and then number them in the order of priority. These will vary from school to school, course to course, and teacher to teacher. You might hit the jackpot and find a job where you inherit a brilliantly resourced department with a treasure trove of a cupboard bursting with well-organized and well-looked-after resources. I've never had this happen to me, by the way. In one job, I found several holdall bags full of absolutely terrifying porcelain dolls, dressed in Victorian costumes and with swivelling heads like Linda Blair in *The Exorcist*. Despite several appeals, their owner never came forward to claim them. In another job, I was the lucky recipient of around 4,000 copies of the novel (not the play text of) *Lord of the Flies*. I did try to offload them to the English department, but they didn't have room for them alongside their stock of 8,000 copies of the book. Flippancy aside, and in an educational climate which is seemingly permanently underfunded, you will need to pick and choose your resources carefully. Some things are going to be non-negotiable. Copies of set texts, for example. If your school asks you to work from photocopies of the original (something I used to see with alarming regularity on my travels as a visiting examiner) then feel free to remind them of the legislation surrounding copyright and that you can't legally photocopy a complete play text.

Let's not forget, as well, the wealth of freely available and digital resources. Most theatres and commercial producers will now provide a free education pack for their production. This is often to lure you into the show itself and make you buy dozens of tickets for your students. It is usually the case that you don't need to have bought tickets for the production to be able to download the education pack from the theatre's website. These education packs typically contain interviews with theatre makers, short essays and ideas for practical activities and exploration of the play and its themes in a practical setting. Make use of these. If they're well written by someone who knows what they are doing, these could prove to be an invaluable and free resource. Likewise, newspaper articles, magazines, podcasts, online video clips and any number of digital resources can be called into service.

Some of the best drama teachers I know manage to be exceptionally creative with limited resources and design their curriculum and assessment in such a way that it meets the needs of their students in the teaching space they have with an assessment model which works for them. These teachers are adept at delivering dynamic lessons which teach the use of theatrical design skills, and always make me renew my vows to deliver more lessons which involve these skills. As previously mentioned, the prominence of theatre design in the current GCSE and A level specifications for our subject is one of the most significant changes seen since the subject was reformed. It is something that we now *have* to get to grips with and take on board, like it or not. Delivering theatre design lessons is where you might really feel the pinch of a limited budget and it is admittedly more challenging to cover these skills – certainly at examination level – if you don't have appropriate resources. You don't necessarily need a room of professional-grade sewing machines, tailors' dummies, mannequins and reams of fabric to be able to deliver costume design. No one is expecting you to be a modern-day Coco Chanel. But you would need to be able to make some sort of costume resources available. The trick here is to think about what you can and can't achieve and perhaps tailor your offerings based on where your students' needs meet your actual resources at the midpoint of this hypothetical Venn diagram. If you feel that you want to make all design skills available to your students, then you need to make sure that appropriate stuff to teach these skills is available. One year, during my annual tour of motorway service stations interspersed with performances of A level drama, I was sent to a pretty remote school in the wilds of Cumbria. A visibly stressed drama teacher met me in the car park and explained that he had done his best with a small handful of children. (Visiting examiners should, at this stage, click into 'smile and nod' mode, a bit like a member of the Royal Family meeting a pop star at the Royal Variety Performance.) He said that the school hadn't given him many resources as they weren't confident that the subject would grow, but that one student had been desperate to provide lighting for the production, and would be assessed accordingly. We went into the performance space so I could be introduced to the students. In all my years of visiting examining, I would walk into a room and be met by a row of seventeen-year-olds who looked like they were about to be put up against a wall and shot. By me. The room I was taken into on this occasion was, in fact, a classroom, and this was also the performance space. Let me clarify: it was a reasonable-sized classroom with large windows through which the evening sunlight streamed. The desks and chairs had been pushed to the back of the room to create a small performance space. The room was lit by fluorescent strip lighting and one single theatre lantern was mounted on a stand, facing the performance space. It was obvious, even before the performance had started, that the lighting effects were going to be limited. They had to be, judging by the absence of resources and equipment. And so it went. I felt that the student who had opted to be assessed on their lighting skills had been short-changed by the school. The dilemma is whether that teacher should have offered lighting in the first place? I would argue not. Think carefully when it comes to what you're offering, whether it's theatre design or other topics. If the appropriate equipment and resources aren't available, it's going to be a stressful and problematic process which is highly unlikely to yield spectacular results. Being creative with a limited budget is one thing. Stretching resources so much that they cease to function is quite another.

Creating work

I mentioned this before, but it's perhaps worth pointing out again, that there is no formal or recognized measurement or scale on which to measure creativity. And yet. At the very heart of our subject, or all artistic subjects and artistic pursuits, is the need to create; to be creative, to make things, to bring things into being which didn't exist before. Drama as a subject is, in and of itself, creative and, by taking part in drama lessons, students can develop their skills in creativity. We must distinguish between the idea of creativity and the 'mere' creation of something. Drama involves the creation, usually of performance, and possibly of some sort of text, too. When we talk about creativity in our subject, though, we need to think about how the practical work that we do can allow works of art to be created, but – and I would argue more importantly – focus on how they will provide opportunities for students to develop their skills in creativity, however we might choose to measure this. What we are looking at here is how a practical experience in a space might develop the potential to work collaboratively and explore themes and ideas to create something which did not exist before. At this abstract level, the notion of creating work and being asked to measure something as potentially ephemeral as creativity might prove daunting. Try to focus on the freedom that this 'filling up of space' provides for you and your students and encourage them to understand the scope provided by the imaginative possibilities when they are asked to create something.

The notion of imagination is crucial here. A few years ago, after a particularly challenging day's teaching and an after-school run-in with a line manager, I decided to work off my frustrations by going and spending money I didn't have on things I didn't need. I am really good at this. A canvas print in an art shop caught my eye. It simply said: *Imagination Is More Important Than Knowledge*. Perfect, I thought. At the risk of appearing both petty and truculent, I'll buy this and hang it in my drama studio so that whenever I next have a 'heated debate' with the aforementioned myopic line manager, I can just point at this quote. A bit of investigation revealed that rather than coming from the world of platitudinous quotes which belong on fridge magnets and 'shabby chic' trinkets, the quote is actually attributed to Albert Einstein. Perfect! If this quote which embraces the very essence of what we drama teachers do is good enough for the world's most renowned physicist, then it's good enough for me. (Side note: I calmed down, the canvas never made it into school, but it is on the wall of my living room to this day.) Einstein is saying – and I love this – that knowledge is limited to the confines of what can be known, whereas imagination offers a broader sweep, a wider scope and the possibility for potentially limitless discovery. If creativity is the car, then imagination is its petrol. Everyone possesses imagination, to some degree or another. Young children, at play, and without many of the constraints or anxieties of social conditioning and expectations, will display imagination and creativity by the bucketload. It is often the case that, as we get older, we are less and less inclined to take the risks required to show how our imagination works and be creative. Consider, then, that it's no coincidence that teenagers become more wary and cautious about how much they show and what they reveal. Right at the time when assessments in drama need them to be able to demonstrate their creative thinking and understanding. Being creative in drama, and being asked to use their imagination to do or make something, can feel like a big risk, and also one which is exposing and can leave students feeling vulnerable.

Imagination needs ideas. Or, at least, for the purposes of teaching drama it needs an idea. In terms of asking students to create something, this will vary in its complexity according to age and level of attainment. What *won't* change is that you are asking students to deliver a finished product, and their starting point is an idea. This idea might take the form of a stimulus. Exam boards love stimuli; they feature in all of the main exam boards' current specifications at all levels. If we give students a stimulus, or a range of stimuli, we can then ask them to practically explore them to see what dramatic potential they might hold. How do you explore stimuli? That depends on the students and the task and what the stimuli might be. Improvisation – with guidance and some sort of imposed structure or set of rules – can often be used to see what ideas an artefact might hold, for example. It's also very useful for us, as teachers, to see how a particular group of students might approach this task and what ideas they might explore or contribute. By seeing *how* our students approach a practical task, we gain a better understanding of who they are as learners. Stimuli can unlock imaginative power and release ideas that students didn't necessarily know that they had in them. What students will need is encouragement and the practical tasks to be broken down into shorter and more manageable chunks. Feedback, suggestions and encouragement will all help. The most important thing is that students are given time and space to contribute and explore their ideas, and also that they feel safe in doing so. The last part cannot be overstated, and a student's ability to overcome any natural inhibitions or fears that they may have is usually key to their success. Through the practical experience of creating work, students can try things out, see what works, and along the way also recognize that not everything is going to work.

Clichéd though it may be, it is entirely true that failure is part of success. Or, rather, that on the pathway to an overall successful outcome or conclusion, there is very likely to be some sort of failure or things that didn't work. When creating work, and especially when guiding students through their creation of work, we can only really define and understand what is successful and what does work in drama by also recognizing and pointing out what *doesn't* work. The rigour of the creative process and especially the 'failures along the way' that come with it risk being demoralizing for students. It's vital that, when we are supporting students as they create practical work of any variety, there are regular checks in place so that a student (or a group of students) doesn't have the chance to stray too far off-piste, or for too long. Build into your curriculum planning 'marker posts' for checking practical work in progress. That might be as simple as you circulating the practical working space once during a lesson where students have twenty minutes to create a small scene. It could extend to frequent and regular checking of devising work, especially at GCSE and A level. To be able to develop and refine their work meaningfully, students need to have opportunities to present it at a 'work in progress' stage in rehearsal, and also receive constructive feedback. There is a bit of hoop-jumping to be aware of on this point. Ofqual regulations and exam boards usually provide definitions about the amount and type of feedback that students are allowed to receive from teachers during the practical creative process. There has to be the opportunity for teachers to give meaningful feedback and support without getting to the point where students are being directed like marionettes. The vocabulary that we use when giving feedback is important and should also mirror and reflect that used when giving any written feedback or whatever levels of attainment you use as a school, or are used by the exam board. The repetition and predictability of the vocabulary we use should become part and parcel of the practical process.

On the other hand, when performing the work, this can also provide ample opportunity for students to receive feedback from their peers. This feedback is usually verbal, though could be in writing, and works twofold because it means that the work in progress gets a trial run and its creators get to see how it is received, whilst the audience has an opportunity to develop skills in analysis and evaluation. It is absolutely the case that students should use the same sort of vocabulary that we do when giving feedback, and that this can deepen the understanding of the assessment process and how the work they are seeing fits into a bigger picture. You don't need me to point out that some students will take pleasure in providing harsh criticism or feedback which borders on the overly picky. Providing some sort of structure and guidance for students to give feedback is important, and students should be pushed to justify and provide evidence for their reasons. Just as they would do if this were a piece of written work. Why place so much emphasis on feedback throughout the creative process? Partly as a reminder, because too often it doesn't happen. The pressures of time and the looming end of each lesson mean that, all too often, we push on with the practical work, desperate for the precious minutes that these students have together where they can collaborate. I can be guilty of this myself, especially when trying to monitor several pieces of group work simultaneously. However, both from observation and from experience, it is absolutely the case that time spent stepping away from the creating to allow some marker-post performance feedback to take place is time well spent. It sharpens the focus, reminds students of their aims and embeds structure and the lexicon of assessment into the process itself. These things can all be easily delivered at the same time, through the practical creative process, saving time and a headache later on.

Practical work, whereby creativity can develop and an end product is created, usually falls into two categories: scripted and devised. Let's look at both.

In terms of scripted work, I've mentioned earlier in this chapter when I think it's best to introduce work on play texts and the different types of resources that are available. Frankly, the world is your oyster. There's a whole separate discussion (of which, more in Chapter 5) to be had about the feasibility and relevance of scripted plays, but we need to consider how best to manage the creative process when scripted work is involved. Picking the right script is about 90 per cent of the battle. Your 'right script' might look different from my 'right script' and I still get it wrong some of the time. Every year, when it comes to thinking about scripts, especially with my GCSE and A level classes, I have a proper think. Reluctant to keep churning out the same plays year on year, I'll look online, think back to recommendations I've seen from friends and from the online drama teaching community, as well as thinking back to what I've seen at the theatre. *What play is going to keep them engaged for ten weeks, offer enough opportunities to get everyone involved and be something they might enjoy?* If I could pay someone to do this job for me every year, I would; it's a tightrope-walking act, for sure. A couple of years ago, a bright and keen group of GCSE students told me they wanted a verbatim play which was challenging, 'gritty', involved multi-roling and would stretch them. I found that play! Michael Wynne's brilliant play (and it really *is* a brilliant play) *Who Cares* ticked all these boxes.

Suddenly, the students' criteria had changed; it wasn't funny enough, there wasn't enough scope for physical theatre, it didn't involve the *type* of multi-roling that they were thinking of. Sigh. Some teachers will allow their students to pick their plays and, where relevant, decide which extracts to rehearse and perform. These teachers clearly have the patience of saints. I've learned from bitter and frustrated experience that this is usually a pathway to stress and failure. Our students don't know as much about drama as we do. They don't know as many plays as we know. Why are we letting them choose which plays they are going to study, especially when this can determine part of an exam result for them? The principle in itself is noble and democratic; let the student be fully involved in their learning. Sure. The reality is that this is fraught with problems. Better, I think, to offer students a small selection of plays that you've vetted and pre-approved. That way, whichever they pick, there is the feeling of choice and ownership on their part as well as security and peace of mind on your part, given that it meets with your initial seal of approval.

During my time as a visiting examiner – and latterly, moderator – it was always very easy to tell by watching a performance which students had enjoyed their text and which students hadn't. Enthusiasm drives commitment and is a key factor in attainment. Students are more likely to do well with work that they feel some sort of a connection to and enjoy. If that sounds obvious, you might be surprised by how many students seem to have been cast and asked to perform in some seriously odd choices. They don't tend to do well. Students who are cast by their teachers in plays and – crucially – in roles which allow them to demonstrate their skills and access the full range of marks available tend to do better than those who have been given a play simply because it 'worked well last year'. Beware of this pitfall. The conundrum of casting is one which is keenly felt, judging by the scores of messages on social media asking for advice and suggestions. If in doubt, play to the students' strengths and cast them as closely to their natural type as possible. Before the GCSE and A level qualifications were reformed, some exam boards sent visiting moderators into schools to work with teachers to standardize and ratify the marks being awarded for practical work. (Ofqual removed this option from exam boards' offerings because it was apparently too unreliable and presented significant challenges in ensuring rigour and authenticity in the marking.) Subtly different from an examiner, but still usually dressed in some sort of snazzy scarf and boots combo, the visiting moderator would watch the performances and then have a conversation with the teacher who would reveal the marks that they wanted to award. (Visiting examiners are not allowed to enter into any discussion about the marking with students, parents or teachers during their visit.) As a moderator, I would sometimes have to encourage teachers to move a proposed mark a little lower or higher to come in line with the nationally agreed standard set by the exam board. On many occasions, where I was suggesting that a student be given a higher mark than that originally proposed by the teacher, I'd hear the teacher remark, '*But … they're just playing themselves*'. This may be the case, but unfamiliar with the student as I am, I haven't met them before and don't know this. There is a strategic cunning and craftiness in casting students in roles which are as much like themselves as possible. If in doubt, with casting for practical work, start with this principle in mind.

Devising work presents its own glorious set of problems and obstacles, all of which can be successfully negotiated by teachers when setting up the practical task for students. Making sure that students stay on track and focused throughout their devising work can be problematic; without the safety net and enforced structure that a script brings, students have the flexibility to go in any direction they like. On the one hand, this encourages creativity and imaginative thinking, as well as collaboration. On the other, the road to devising success is littered with the carcasses of failed attempts, mistakes and ideas which were cast aside on the journey. It is inherently challenging for students to agree on a collective style of working, shared aims and how to get there. If they aren't all willing to move in the same direction, the opportunities for creativity to flourish diminish significantly. Clear and non-negotiable guidance for students at the outset of the practical devising project is paramount. Make sure that they understand their final deadline as well as marker-post targets along the way. I have always been an advocate of each working group drawing up their own working charter, where they set their rules for the devising process which they need to abide by. Publish them. Make sure everyone has a copy. And stick to them. Whether it's small children being asked to make up a play or a professional company who specializes in devising original work, no one finds this process easy. But it can be enormously rewarding and satisfying.

At exam level, students will be expected to reflect and give an account of their process and performance. To start with, they will need to state their aims, be these individual, collective or both. Get them written down. It's fine (and typical) if these aims change during the process and the final product doesn't resemble what it was supposed to at the start. We've all seen the piece which was going to tell the story of the women at Greenham Common and morphed into a biography of Amy Winehouse somewhere along the way. Make sure that your students keep a regularly updated record of what it is that they *do* during the process, as well as the feedback that they are given. These notes can easily form the basis of their revision materials and will provide an individualized account of the journey and how the process defined the outcome. I've seen teachers be really creative with this. Some students upload all of their notes to a centralized blog or electronic file which all of the group can access. Other students, especially those who struggle with literacy, create voice notes which they save and refer back to. In many schools, the devising process is becoming increasingly paper-free. Think about which method will work best for your students. As long as the process is captured in some way, you'll stand more chance of making purposeful reference to it later.

In terms of devising, the practical process tends to become more difficult to negotiate as students progress through the levels of attainment. At Key Stage 3, you can create your own success criteria, of course. By the time students have reached GCSE, there might be an expectation to work in a specific theatrical style or genre. This can provide challenges for students because it makes further demands of them, but it can be useful for us as teachers, especially when it comes to providing feedback or assessing the work. It's quite easy to demonstrate or model the hallmarks of Epic Theatre or Commedia dell'arte as a discrete task and then ask students to implement these in their devising work. Then, when you're giving feedback of practical work during the creative process, you can see if these hallmarks are included or not. It's often the case that a limp or stodgy scene can be revitalized by reworking it with a particular stylistic feature; the group's collective focus can be both refreshed and refined. At A level, theatrical practitioners (which can include companies) will also need to be implemented, and students' work will need to make clear reference to the stylistic features of practitioners, or their influence. Some exam boards are much more didactic than others in this respect. By this stage, the challenge for us as teachers in supporting students through the practical process is to ensure suitability of stimulus, style, practitioner and a focus on the overall task and target. Following the qualification reforms, at GCSE and A level, students cannot be awarded any credit by teachers for the practical work that they do as part of the creative process. So all of the good work which might be done at this stage is to hopefully create a strong piece for performance, as well as points of reference for post-event analysis, reflection and evaluation. As good (or otherwise) as this process may prove, the process in and of itself isn't marked. Consider that if, for example, twelve weeks are spent using every lesson for rehearsal time, creating a devised performance, it is the comparatively brief performance itself that is marked. As I have progressed through my teaching career, I have realized that however long I give my students is enough. If I give them four weeks, the process will take them exactly that long. Should I give them an entire term, the creative process will take the full term. And either way there will be the same dithering about ideas, hesitation about which direction to take, and those words which can curdle any drama teacher's blood the week before the performance: 'We've decided to change what our piece is about.' Resist this, and encourage groups to work through their existing material, however limited or weak it might be, and try to salvage what is usable and build upon that, rather than a complete reboot.

Two final thoughts about the devising process. The process yields the very best results and truly nurtures and develops creativity when it is at its most practical. When students are up on their feet, exploring and trying things out and seeing what happens. Whether it's due to laziness or a tendency to over-intellectualize the process, students can be inclined to think through the ideas rather than try them out. Thinking the ideas through won't reveal whether they have any merit or traction, or otherwise. Getting up off chairs and putting the idea through some sort of practical exploration *will* show whether it has potential. Oddly, the most academic students I have taught (and, therefore, the ones who are likely to achieve the highest overall grades) are less good at devising, less inclined to take risks and less willing to practically explore an idea, when compared to my least academic students. Something about the discussion and thinking-through of the ideas is the death knell for real creativity when students are devising. '*Will such and such an idea work?*' my students will frequently ask me. '*I have no idea*', I tell them, slowly losing the will to live. '*Why not GET UP OFF YOUR CHAIRS AND TRY IT OUT?*' The last part is bellowed with encouragement and in a caring tone, I'm sure you'll understand.

The final trick I've learned over my years of nurturing the next generation's Sally Cooksons and Simon McBurneys through the practical devising process is to create your own list of 'Embargoed Themes, Topics and Ideas'. I don't know what you're sick of seeing, or whether there are other more legitimate academic reasons for steering students away from a particular idea. But do not be afraid to do so. I used to start the devising project by showing my students examples of successful, completed devised pieces from the previous academic year's cohort. Especially the ones which displayed real creativity, ingenuity or moments of brilliance. The downfall with this, I realized, is that students are mimetic and I was starting to see pale and reductive photocopied versions of the work that I had shown them. Now I only show them carefully selected clips rather than a full piece. Model the technique, or the idea, rather than laying out the full narrative for them. My Embargo List changes and waxes and wanes from time to time, depending on my mood and what my students produce, but there are some mainstays. I don't ever want to see any devised pieces which include: candles, dolls, possessed dolls, dolls in Victorian costumes, nursery rhymes, slowly sung nursery rhymes, nursery rhymes which are slowly sung by possessed dolls by candlelight, witches, green witches, references to *Wicked*, flashback sequences in red lighting, gameshows, adverts, physical theatre sequences which do not enhance mood or character or story, pieces in which the final scene includes the line, 'And it was all in her head the entire time', Donald Trump, Brexit, the life and times of Katie Price. As well as limiting what they cannot do, remember that the stimulus you give your students (if you're the one who gets to choose the stimulus rather than an exam board) is critical and that the end product is likely to be informed and shaped by whatever it was that the group set out with. Yes, as I said, it's a minefield. By the time I've done some scripted work with a group, I'm always keen to get started on some devising, and vice versa. That's just the way it goes. Keeping them focused whilst preserving our own sanity is the real challenge.

Performing

At the heart of drama or theatre is performance. Whether this is the smallest children taking part in their first school nativity play, right through to sophisticated graduate-level work, and into the theatre profession itself, most people are drawn to our subject because of a love of performance. The performance of drama is, in its essence, the same as it was in the first recorded performances. As a communal experience, the observing and watching of other people pretending, dressing up, playing, trying to convince us that they are what they aren't, is a departure from the everyday. If we are asking students to perform their work to an audience (of some sort) then we are continuing this ages-old tradition. Drama, as an art form, as most people understand it lives or dies by performance. There is a continuing debate amongst drama teachers about whether the subject is 'a practical subject' or not, and what proportion of any assessment or attainment should come from practical work. Comparisons are often made to Art in this respect, but it's not a particularly useful comparison. A GCSE or A level qualification in Art (it might be Art and Design, or Graphic Design) poses a set of demands for its students which focuses on their creative development, as well as what they create. It is assessed in an entirely different way to the equivalent qualifications in Drama, or Drama and Theatre, as it is at A level. Whereas an Art qualification is made up of a portfolio, developed over time, and then a final assessment, both of which are about the application and demonstration of acquired practical skills, our subject makes demands of its students which cover more skills sets. As well as performing, we have to teach our students how to work collaboratively, understand the work of professional theatre makers, analyse and evaluate their own work, show an appreciation of live performance work, develop their understanding of the role of the director, create their own work from scratch, study theatre history and apply their own understanding of theatrical practitioners. Throughout all this, performance remains at the core; all roads lead to and from performance.

When students get to perform in our lessons they have the chance to demonstrate their skills and their creativity, and they have to do this with people watching them, ready to critique them. When our subject is compulsory as part of a student's curriculum, it becomes clearer to see those who enjoy performance and those who think it's some sort of archaic punishment. By the time students opt for drama, as they progress through their school career, it is more and more likely to appeal to those who are good performers. When I say perform, this might mean contributing to a performance as a director or with design skills which embellish and enhance the work on stage. More often than not, though, it's about acting and students gain their best understanding of text and how acting skills are applied by experiential practice. When students have to write about how they might demonstrate their practical skills as part of a written exam it is always the case that they will find the response easiest and be able to write in detail and clarity if they have experienced this work for themselves. Any theories about performance are best tested, explored and demonstrated through performance. For students to stand a chance of falling in love with our subject, it is usually because of a performance; theirs or someone else's. And this is all before we consider how performance work can be vital to us as subject teachers. We get to know and understand our students best when we watch them perform. We can detect their sense of pride, see their confidence grow, perhaps notice their anxieties and nerves and vulnerability. Not only can we use performance work to help 'road test' play texts or see how a devised piece works in reality (rather than in theory, in rehearsal) but the performance of drama work is also an essential assessment tool.

The mark distribution curves of performance work at GCSE and A level don't fit the typical bell-curve model. Instead, there's a sort of snow drift shape which is in favour of the higher end of the assessment scale. As a rule, students love to perform. Whatever nervous energy they might display, it's infinitely preferable to the trudge and chore of rehearsals. It's essential that students, at whatever level, understand how we are using their performance to assess them and what criteria we are using to do this. Whether it's under full stage lighting or the demonstration of a work in progress in a classroom setting, we can measure progress made, assess the demonstration of skills (in line with the brief given) and make a judgement about a student's creativity, all at the same time.

When students are performing scripted work, the assessment made must be in line with the demands presented by the script and the inherent challenges it presents. Whether we are judging the diction, clarity and observance of iambic pentameter when a student performs a speech from *Othello* or considering the physical skills used to bring to life a section of Mark Ravenhill's *pool (no water)*, we can use the performance to make a judgement about how much progress a student has made. What can they do now, at the end of the process, that they couldn't do at the start? When exam boards are assessing students, they aren't concerned about progress made; the board (or their representatives) never saw the students at the start of the process. However, as ongoing subject teachers, we *do* need to consider progress being made. At the risk of stating the obvious, it's our job to support students and enable their progress. Which is a very different thing to delivering an outstanding, final performance. We must also be very clear when we are assessing performance work what it is that we are looking for. It is entirely valid and, indeed, good practice to use a performance of a work in progress or a final performance, to make a judgement on effort made and see how much progress a student has made. We can also use a separate assessment scale but the same performance to make a judgement on a student's demonstration of practical skills.

In terms of presenting devised work, the performance of the final piece, the outcome, is the reason that everyone is there in the first place. Without the performance of the piece, the process itself is meaningless. Having a looming performance date can be an excellent motivational tool. Speaking from experience it is also the date which I end up virtually screaming about as it approaches and my students seem to think that they can complete 50 per cent of the work involved in the last 10 per cent of the rehearsal time. Students are always going to be like this. We can create schedules and targets and wish for it to be different, but the reality is that people (not just students, all people) work to deadlines and will leave things right up to that deadline. At the same time, we need to be firm and non-negotiable about deadlines. I've seen teachers having a really hard time of it when they have started a project without announcing the deadline at the start of the process or not reinforcing it enough. Don't allow students to push or negotiate deadlines for performance with you, especially when it comes to devised work. For the development of work and to satisfy all manner of assessments, performances are not only the best way to focus a collective but also easy to capture as evidence of several students at one time and in one place. We can record a performance and refer back to it, making summative assessment even more straightforward.

When it comes to GCSE and A level qualifications, performance still makes up a significant proportion of a student's attainment. More often than not, teachers wish that performance was worth *more* as part of these qualifications, but – at the time of writing – they are fixed in alignment with Ofqual's reformed subject content and aren't going to budge. Whereas classroom and rehearsal performances can be used for all manner of things, the performances of scripted and devised work as part of these qualifications are there to make a singular judgement on skills demonstrated. These performances might be assessed by you, as is usually the case with devised work, or they may be subject to assessment from a visiting examiner from the exam board. I had this role for many years, and I loved it. Each year I would see devised performances which were entirely original and thought-provoking, as well as seeing scripted work which was moving, thrilling and inspiring. Not all of it was top drawer, of course, but there was always some great stuff out there. Examiners are in short supply and exam boards are always in need of subject teachers to fill these roles. If it's possible to fit this role into your life, do it, without hesitation. No, it won't make you a millionaire, and you'll probably end up having a car floor littered with empty sandwich packets and bottles of water as you make your way from centre to centre. What you will gain is confidence in applying assessment criteria and absolutely loads of experience of doing so. Furthermore, you'll encounter plays and practitioners and ideas for devising which you might not have considered before. Ultimately you will be able to provide better support for your own students. It is the best CPD that you can undertake.

It's also important to think about the role that the audience plays in the performances that you facilitate. Students might groan and panic at the thought of an audience, any audience, especially one with their family and friends. Akin to the *If a tree falls in a forest and no one is there, does it make a sound?* question, I wonder whether a performance without an audience is actually a performance at all. (I'm saying it isn't, but feel free to disagree.) Performances or those snapshot performances of work in progress in lesson time will typically be performed for the rest of the class, the students' peers. It is essential that, rather than just being passive spectators, the audience here has a function as observers ready to give constructive criticism in these situations. Beyond this, the choice is yours and people take very different approaches. As an examiner, I've sat in a packed theatre with around 300 people watching one understandably petrified student deliver a monologue. I'd suggest that more intimate, shorter performances such as monologues and duologues are best served in a smaller performance space with a limited audience of familiar faces who have seen the work in rehearsal. This can create an intimate and reassuring environment. Conversely, longer group performances tend to benefit from an invited audience, especially where comedic pieces are concerned. You can always stage a separate performance for the parents and friends of students after the exam itself if you want to celebrate the performance work without the added pressures of the assessment taking place in front of family members. During my years examining, it was always thrilling to see teachers taking calculated risks with the way that performances were staged. I have marked work that has been performed in site-specific venues and in promenade, as a video camera trailed the performers (to capture evidence of the performance for the exam board) and I have scribbled notes moving from place to place. When the innovation that British theatre has seen in the last thirty years trickles down to students in schools, it is a welcome reminder of how our profession plays its part in inspiring the next generation of theatre makers.

A final point about performance. Live performance work is frightening and exhilarating all at once, and when students are willing to put themselves in such an exposed environment and demonstrate what they can do and what they are good at, it's humbling. We must celebrate performance work wherever possible. If it's appropriate to share the performance work with the school community or the wider community, do so. Schedule your work as far in advance as possible and make sure your senior management team and governors know when it's on. Invite them to be part of the audience; to share in and celebrate your students' success and also see what it is that you do and what you're good at. If your senior management team don't come and watch the work that you do, it's sending a very clear message about how much they do – or don't – value our subject, and they're missing out. But so are the students. They're missing out on support and feeling valued and that the subject they've chosen and the work that they do are an important and integral part of their school community. Surely it isn't too much that our leaders, whose decisions and values define our school community, come and see for themselves what their own colleagues and students can do? If I'm labouring this point it's because it is sadly the case that performance work isn't seen and celebrated by senior leaders in schools. All too often, as an examiner, I would see a brilliant but stressed teacher trying to coordinate the exam performance work, smile and nod at parents and keep their students calm and controlled. With not a member of the senior leadership team in sight. Our subject takes passion, knowledge, skill and hard work just to guide our students through a performance exam. Let's not be shy in asking those who have the most influence in our schools to set aside an hour of their lives to see exactly what it is that we do. Who knows? They might even enjoy it. (They might not, too. I remember a very senior colleague sighing and looking at his watch through most of the second half of a production of *Spring Awakening* I directed many years ago.)

Responding

Finally, as it's all about to come full circle in terms of what we deliver and how we deliver it: responding. The last logical step of the creative process, and what all meaningful creative endeavour should involve, is a period of reflection. This also applies when we, or students, are audience members and have to deliver some sort of critical or evaluative response. There are shelves of libraries and bookshops dedicated specifically to theatre criticism and critical theory. Sidestepping the thorny argument about theatre criticism and whether it is an art form and profession under threat of extinction, as drama teachers we need to focus on analytical and evaluative skills. Students need to know how to respond to work; that doesn't mean they are taught what their response should be or that there is a singularly correct response (I was furious with a right-wing colleague of mine some years ago who took a group of students to see *Billy Elliot: The Musical* and spent the train journey home telling them that it was appalling, blasphemous and offensive, not least in its portrayal of Margaret Thatcher) but that they know how to 'read' what they are seeing and formulate some sort of opinion. Or, that they can self-reflect and apply their own analytical and critical vocabulary to themselves and their own work. Please don't skip over this part of the creative process. I'd be hard pushed to argue that it's just as important as the performance itself, but it's not far behind. Understanding how and why elements of performance work succeed or fail is an important part of any student's education in drama and having a sense of what they need to do to improve their own practice. We need to think about the different ways in which students can be expected to respond to work, and how we can make them a valuable part of our teaching practice.

Firstly, verbal feedback. Students can be asked to give feedback on the work of their peers, and this should become commonplace and part of day-to-day lessons at Key Stage 3. It should become a logical next step for students that, once they have seen some practical work, they are expected to provide a response to it. We might call it feedback or 'tips for improvement' but it's a critical response nonetheless. Students should be told what it is that they are to be evaluating before they watch the work; this needs to be more specific than just 'the performance' and should focus on a particular aspect or aspects of what they are about to see. As teachers, it is our responsibility to provide context for what they are going to watch. Students will also need to know the criteria for success, as this provides a structure and framework for the sort of feedback that they might give. In Chapter 2, I advocated that it is worth building in your own chosen critical vocabulary from an early stage and that this becomes part of the students' discourse. I always ask my students to notice the positive but also consider what room for improvement there might be, and try to get them to deliver this in a constructive way. If a student can successfully apply a set of criteria to a piece of performance work and deliver an evaluative verdict, then they have successfully 'read' that performance. 'Reading' a performance, or making sense of what is seen on a stage (which can be delivered as semiotics at a much higher level), needs to be modelled. We need to show our students how we respond to work and deliver verbal feedback, using the same framework and vocabulary. Delivering feedback verbally isn't just reserved for the work of others; students can be asked to critique their own work (though this is arguably much harder than commenting on the work of others) or the work of theatre makers in practice. As previously discussed in Chapter 2, live theatre-going is now a staple of the GCSE and A level specifications, so any work which can be done lower down the school to support a response to live theatre is emphatically a good thing. Encourage students to volunteer their opinions when giving verbal feedback in a group discussion, but it's imperative that these opinions can also be substantiated and make reference to specific details. If students become used to being asked to substantiate their verbal responses, then this will be easier to manage when trying to coax a written response from them.

Which leads us neatly on to written feedback. The most effective use of written feedback that I have deployed is by placing targeted questionnaires on audience members' chairs and asking them to fill them in throughout the performance. This way, I can simply divide up the responses to give to the relevant groups and they have some ready-made feedback. Students can keep a physical record of their feedback (I might omit anything particularly negative or bleak at this stage) and reflect further on their own practical work. Students themselves will need to develop their skills in written responses, and this becomes more important as they get older. It is a requirement of exam board specifications that students are able to analyse and evaluate their own work as well as the work of others. This is a tall order and it's no surprise that, as teachers have adapted to the new exam specifications, this has become one of the most challenging areas for everyone in the room. There is significant emphasis on providing feedback on the work of others and this tends to mean the work of theatre makers in performance. Like lightning in a bottle, a performance can whizz by, and students can be enthusiastic and positive about what they have seen … but not really remember enough detail about it to be able to generate a coherent response.

Understanding how to structure a response which consists of written feedback or evaluation is a skill which takes time and patience. Students are usually better at describing what they see than they are at providing an analysis of its effects or an evaluation of its success. To enable students to make proper progress, we need to reinforce the vocabulary of analysis and evaluation and help to develop their skills in structuring this sort of feedback. I have found published theatre reviews extremely useful to help support this task. Some of the best arts journalists in the country (and Quentin Letts) are demonstrating how to 'read' a performance and structure their own considered written response in theatre reviews. Students aren't expected to craft theatre *reviews* as such (although it's a worthwhile homework task) but they can be used to highlight where analysis and evaluation takes place and model the vocabulary used to do so. Again, building this into the cycle and making it a regular part of the practical process is key.

Developing a critical vocabulary is an essential part of the response to work seen, and this takes time. Your expectations of a Year 8 class watching a short performance clip on video would be somewhat different to an A level revision class discussing a piece of challenging contemporary theatre. What would remain the same would be the need to give detail and clarity and provide colour to what's written by integrating a proper critical vocabulary. These words could, for example, be displayed on the studio or classroom wall. They might be provided on lists which students can then annotate and augment with words and phrases of their own. Yes, describing something as '*good*' or '*really boring*' does qualify as a critical response; though the limited vocabulary is reductive and doesn't reveal enough about the work seen or the opinion of the individual audience member. Better, then, to encourage verbal discussion which deploys critical vocabulary so its familiarity becomes commonplace. I try to encourage my own students to praise and, to fulfil a cliché, accentuate the positive. The reasoning being is that it's easier to be enthusiastic and talk in detail about what *did* happen than try to write about what wasn't good or went wrong or *didn't* happen. More fulfilling, surely, to write about something that is there than something that isn't. Students will have more to say about what they enjoyed, though be careful of too much hyperbole in any sort of critical response. Years of exam paper marking in the summer months ('No, I'm fine, you go and enjoy yourselves at the barbecue and then the pub beer garden without me; I'll be sitting here marking exam papers') have occasionally thrown up the odd memorable critical response. They don't happen often but now and again a student who's been lucky enough to see a genuine theatrical titan in performance will attempt to write a corrosive and negative critique of how they didn't '*make proper use of their facial expressions*'. Please do encourage your students to be enthusiastic without gushing and develop a critical vocabulary to respond to the very best bits of what they have seen.

Finally, once the work has been created and performed, and some sort of response has been delivered, the true reflective process poses a cyclical sort of question for students: *What would I do differently if I were to do it again?* Try and remove all existential connotations from that query, as well as the image of someone on their death bed, and see it as a question of hope and a wish to improve. At the end of every period of creativity or creative endeavour, reflection is important, and the best way to think about how something might be improved is to think about ways to improve it. Students always find it easier to make improvements and adjustments to something which exists in the first place rather than starting from scratch. Work with this. By taking part in and completing the full creative process (Create – Perform – Respond; at one time the title of this book) students should have gained significant insight into how they work, how they collaborate, how their skills have developed and how they are now more adept at refining and shaping their own work. A colleague and I always used to remark that by the time our A level students had completed their devising process and performance, they had acquired just about enough understanding and experience to make a new start and go back to the beginning. If time allows, build mini projects into your curriculum planning so that students gain an understanding of the shape of the road, as it were. With my own GCSE students, for example, I always make them undertake a short devising project before we start the real work. This way we can identify pitfalls and see how people work best in combination with one another. Frankly, it's a constantly evolving jigsaw without a picture on the lid of the box; we don't always know what the finished product is going to look like. What we can do, though, is be rigorous. And not in the way that you-know-who meant. I mean by us being supportive and nurturing as our pupils create, and understand that they will get things wrong and mistakes will be made along the way. Whether we are picking texts or thinking about stimuli for devising, we must be there to provide buffers for their creative process with regular feedback that makes use of an evolving set of critical vocabulary. Finally, we must celebrate the work in performance, take a step back from it, stroke our chins and ask ourselves how we might improve it. Create. Perform. Respond. It's what Euripides did. Shakespeare worked in that way. Caryl Churchill (surely the greatest living playwright) does the same. It's at the heart of our subject and I can't see that changing. We would all be the poorer if it did change.

4

Surviving: The pressure points

'A soft subject'

'What will she actually be able to do with a GCSE in Drama?'
'I've heard that the subject is entirely practical. Is that true?'
I know that lots of universities won't accept A level Drama, which is why I'm worried about him taking it.'
'Is the subject more than just about building confidence?'
'It's not very academic, though, is it?'
'I just don't think it's going to help her if she takes a soft subject.'

Let's play 'drama teacher bingo' for a moment and see how many of those phrases you've heard from parents, students or colleagues during your time teaching the subject. Most of us will have heard all of these, or slight variants, before we have finished our NQT year. Charming. Do our colleagues in other subjects hear these sort of things? I would suggest that they don't, or at least not to the same degree. I don't believe that there is any other academic subject on a school's curriculum which is subject to such misinformation, lack of understanding and – occasionally, sadly – mockery and ridicule. Even our fellow creative bedfellows like Art and Music don't tend to attract such wary suspicion or a complete failure to understand what our subject delivers in terms of transferable skills and why it is both brilliant and essential for any student. Frankly, it's a nonsense that this is the case. However, now that we have looked at your curriculum and assessment design and how this might work in reality, it's time to focus on the things that get in the way and the hurdles and obstacles that are part and parcel of the delivery of our subject. These are likely to be the issues which can cause stress or conflict and which create pressure. It's worth thinking about them in advance to have an idea of how to tackle them when they arise.

Of course, in an ideal world, we wouldn't have to defend our subject. In the real world, however, 'twas ever thus. The only way that we will ever reach a situation where we *don't* have to present the case for the defence is if, as a community of drama teachers, we use facts and evidence to politely set the misinformed on the proverbial straight and narrow. When it comes to defending the subject against accusations that it is 'soft' or 'not an academic subject' or 'not a proper subject', let's remember that those definitions in themselves are meaningless and often wrongly applied.

A soft subject is, by definition, not a 'hard subject', yet the latter is a phrase which I don't ever remember hearing. Core subjects, yes. STEM subjects, of course. Never, though, are subjects labelled as 'hard'. Quite right, too. Different subjects offer different things and in different ways, so the definitions of them as hard or soft are meaningless. Some people will naturally find things more challenging than others. If we dig a little deeper, it seems to make even less sense. Hard subjects or soft subjects seem to be characterized by the skills sets which they cover in their delivery. Hard skills are defined as the set of skills which you need to do a job. These skills are repeatedly defined as teachable and measurable, and examples given frequently include reading, writing, mathematical ability or, at a higher level, things such as web design, accountancy and financial skills and computer programming. Whilst creativity will naturally be a component of any job role, the creative impulse or any sort of artistry seems to be absent from these definitions and examples. The reason this definition is fraudulent is that arguably none or very few of these skills would be needed to be an actor, as an example. Yet the skills that you *do* need to become an actor are teachable and measurable. It's also entirely possible to teach and measure all sorts of skills sets associated with drama and theatre. And yet. Our subject is thought to be a soft subject, because it apparently focuses on soft skills. These are slightly harder to pin down and somewhat esoteric in their collective definition. Soft skills are usually thought to focus on the ability to communicate, to work well as part of a team and adapt, to be creative, or to display emotional intelligence. All of these are part of what we deliver as drama teachers and often they present themselves organically within what we deliver and how we deliver it. My argument has always been that the wealth of (if you want to call them) soft skills that our subject enables is an attractive and valuable addition to its core skills in literacy, comprehension, understanding and (eventually, at GCSE and A level) analysis and evaluation. To successfully structure an essay on how *Macbeth* uses the supernatural, or why Marlene in *Top Girls* is a critique of the materialism of 1980s Thatcherite Britain in action, requires a combination of skills which are routinely classified as hard *and* soft. Drama is not a soft subject. It can't be because it contains too many attributes and hallmarks of what are thought to be hard skills. If we fail to point this out whenever it may arise, and if we don't create a clear and robust defence of what we do, then we risk being patronized, isolated and undervalued as a subject.

If creativity is impossible to measure (which it is), why is it labelled as a soft skill? I don't have the answer to that question, and don't seek to change generations of thinking about which skills are hard and soft. What I would argue, though, is that creativity in itself is very challenging to teach and requires in-depth specialist knowledge and experience. Furthermore, the measurement or assessment of that creativity needs to take place on an invented scale of measurement somehow. It isn't routine, is often unpredictable and the variety of what we deliver can make it a challenge to assess these soft skills. The fact that drama teachers' work is largely focused on what are thought to be soft skills is surely cause for our collective celebration. What we do, day in and day out, can often be harder than some of the things which are routinely delivered in other subjects. Don't get me wrong. I have every respect for our fellow colleagues in other subjects and could no more hope to deliver a successful Physics or French lesson than I could hope to levitate and fly to the moon. What we do is different and highly specialized, and we need to collectively work to stamp out misconceptions, have pride in what we do and make sure that the message we send to our school communities is one which shows what it is that we are about. This is emphatically not about generating competition between subjects, but about spreading a better understanding of what we do. That starts with promoting our subject as one which enhances creativity and harnesses all sorts of so-called soft skills, but demonstrating that it's a subject which has developed significantly over the last forty years and now stands shoulder to shoulder with other academic subjects.

Let's not be scared of promoting our subject as academic. It is. It's also creative and fun and exciting and can engage learners in a way that some other subjects can't. Music, at GCSE and at A level, is constructed in exactly the same way as drama, including practical work, different methods of assessment and formal written exams. Music is sometimes thought of as being 'more academic' than drama. This isn't the case; these creative subjects are comparable, highly valuable as a qualification and – guess what – academic. A couple of years ago, I was interviewed by a doctorate student compiling research about drama in schools and academia. At the end of the interview, where I had banged on and on about how much our subject can be undervalued and whether we practitioners truly do enough to promote its academic value, she said that I was the only person she had interviewed who had suggested that the subject was 'inherently academic', whereas most of my colleagues had highlighted the recent reforms in the subject and a supposed lack of emphasis on practical work. To be clear about this, the reform of drama at GCSE and A level has increased the amount of assessments that students take and decreased the amount of work which is able to be assessed via performance or practical work. That much is unambiguous, but there is a misconception which has become commonplace that the delivery of the subject and our lessons themselves are now much less practical on a day-to-day basis. From my own perspective, my own lessons have remained as practical as they ever were; students need heaps of time focused on practical experience before they can then begin to process and write about this experience. Whatever the most recent subject reform has brought in terms of changes to our subject, and whatever future reforms may bring, the subject remains rooted in practical experience. It is not a contradiction that our subject is both practical and academic.

My own headteacher when I was at secondary school used to cheerfully refer to GCSE drama as 'lessons where we pretend to be trees' and A level drama as 'lessons where we pretend to be trees in a breeze'. Tactfully sidestepping any of the institutionalized problems which statements like that reveal, this is an example of the sort of 'good-natured' teasing that we often have to endure as drama teachers. Most of these remarks, typically made by our own colleagues, are made in jest. We need to be aware, though, that misconception can still exist when it comes to our subject and this can prove increasingly problematic if it isn't dealt with. Some of my own A level students recently noticed that a leading British university had posted online a list of subjects which they would consider as part of an A level profile of prospective applicants and another list of subjects which weren't allowed. Music appeared on the former list, whilst Drama appeared on the latter, which caused some genuine concern for some of my students. I phoned the university and spoke to their admissions office (and it isn't the first time that I have done this) and asked them for a justification for this, pointing out that music is an art form assessed in *exactly* the same way as drama at A level. A couple of conversations and emails with the relevant people and Drama was added to the 'allowed' list. Which is exactly as it should be. I'm not suggesting that an occasional tease from colleagues about the inherently practical nature of our subject leads directly to universities disallowing our subject at A level for no apparently logical reason. But this is all part and parcel of the same situation. Drama is not a soft subject.

A trick I learned a few years back, working in a sixth form college where lots of students progressed straight into employment or apprenticeships rather than into universities and higher education, was to look at what employers were looking for when it came to recruiting staff. This was revelatory and won the argument for me, faced with a cynical group of students, worried that their A level in Drama and Theatre Studies was going to be a waste of time. Employers genuinely value people who can work successfully through collaboration or teamwork. Similarly, employees who are confident and able to communicate and listen to others are highly sought-after. At GCSE and A level, drama improves time-keeping and students' abilities in how to solve problems, often with creative or lateral thinking. Words and phrases such as these often feature in job adverts, or the 'person specification' of a job application pack. If faced with the Doubting Thomases (and Doubting Traceys, for balance), feel free to point them in the direction of job websites.

Finally, consider the graduates of drama schools. By no means a full and complete representation of our subject in the academic world (though most drama schools' qualifications are now allied to a university), drama school graduates are highly trained and specialized and ready to work in the world of performing arts. The snag is that there are many more qualified (and unqualified) potential artistes than there are jobs. A recent survey of drama school graduates found that, for around 90 per cent of their time, qualified actors are unemployed. Or rather, they are not in paid employment in acting work. A different study by Queen Mary University in London revealed that only 2 per cent of qualified actors 'make a living' from the acting profession. These are grim statistics, and it is always hard to strike a balance between inspiring our students who dream of being the next Cynthia Erivo or Noel Clarke and at the same time giving them a fair dose of the realities of what is a really tough profession. The point here is that these graduates have to try and find employment in sectors which aren't to do with the performing arts, and this is where the diversity of their skills set will become important. All of the transferable skills, acquired and refined through study at school and beyond, become invaluable and a lifeline to being able to afford a living. More often than not, it is the so-called soft skills which graduates can most meaningfully deploy to help them gain employment. Yes, our subject is doing much more than training actors and has many more routes of progression than drama school, but the transferable skills and the skills set itself are what helps to create value (in the non-fiscal sense) and makes drama a subject to cherish and to champion.

Cross-curricular understanding

Having touched upon potential 'banter' between colleagues in other departments, it's worth considering ways in which we can avoid friction between colleagues. This is an avoidable source of stress and our subject can be used in conjunction with our colleagues in other subjects to have a genuine and meaningful impact on students. I use the word 'impact' purposefully; this is a buzzword increasingly popular with Ofsted, our friendly inspectorate body, and ISI, the independent schools' equivalent. As teachers, we are now expected to measure progress, chart this progress and prove how our students are learning and making this progress. The impact that we make as teachers is now more important than ever, provided that you buy into the notion that Ofsted inspections are vital, purposeful and absolutely essential, as I clearly do. Brushing aside any slightly sarcastic undertones, if we think about impact in terms of bringing about potential innovation and exciting change with students, it is worth thinking about what we do and how our subject can be enhanced by other subjects, and vice versa, aiming for maximum impact. At this stage, it's worth considering not just the skills that our subject can facilitate but the way that our subject can be used as a medium, a way to deliver the content of other subjects.

Part of this involves potentially demystifying what goes on inside the drama studio. It's not magic or sorcery, and we are always following established processes, but to some of our colleagues the drama teaching space can be daunting and something to avoid, especially if put on a drama cover lesson. I understand this in reverse; if I'm asked to cover a colleague's lesson in a regular classroom, I find the relative lack of open space odd. The rows of desks and chairs and the reliance on books and writing are unusual and feel unfamiliar. Being asked to cover a lesson on a sports pitch is something which feels *more* terrifying. In an even more unfamiliar environment, I don't know what the rules are, I'm not sure what 'normal' is and I think I'm going to get everything wrong. Consider, then, how non-subject specialist teachers might feel upon entering the drama studio space and the fear (perhaps an overstatement) that this might provoke. All that empty space, lighting equipment, costumes and a lack of desks and chairs. Perfect for us, a nightmare for others. How many of us have also had the experience of a member of senior management popping their head into our lesson and looking confused or aghast at groups of student in full throttle rehearsal mode? To them it can look like unregulated chaos and noise, whereas we see it as a well-organized rehearsal space for multiple groups, all on task and rehearsing for an upcoming performance. We can make a great impact on students if we can bring other subjects into our learning space, and vice versa.

Whenever I'm required to teach a Greek drama, and it's usually to a class of A level students, I have a brief pang of panic. Yes, I promise I know Greek drama; I did it at school and at university and I've successfully taught many of the texts to students who didn't fail. But every year, possibly due to not delivering this material very often, I feel all at sea and have to book myself on to a self-taught refresher course. It was the kind offer of a colleague in my school's Classics department that changed things for me. I'd confessed my periodic fear with classical texts and she generously offered to take one of my lessons and explain the nuts and bolts of Greek performance and the origins of the terminology. In return, she suggested that I could take one of her lessons and give her students an understanding of these texts as a blueprint for performance rather than a historical artefact. This meant, in reality, something like a well-received theory lesson for my lot and a 'desks to the side of the room' practical drama session for her gang. It absolutely worked. I'd used my subject to make a real impact on students of my colleague's subject, and vice versa. Of course, you couldn't work like this all the time, continually swapping lessons and hoping to make an impact around the school. But the fact is that there are often more points of commonality between our subjects and our colleagues' subjects than we realize. The trick is to find the point of crossover and work from there.

There is also a difference between using our skills to facilitate the delivery of other subjects and using our subject to deliver curricular content from other areas. Drama teachers can often have seemingly random but deep pockets of information about specific historical periods, incidents or people from history. For example, I know plenty about Captain James Cook's crossing to Botany Bay in Australia in 1770 and the establishment of a penal colony there because I've taught Timberlake Wertenbaker's masterpiece *Our Country's Good* several times. Why is it that I'm aware of the intricate details of the founding of the American financial system and how this was born out of struggle? Because I've taught the musical *Hamilton*. These are highly specialized areas of interest; the sort of things that would normally be the answers to questions on *Mastermind* or *University Challenge*. But when they've been dissected and repackaged as easily consumable and entertaining pieces of drama, the details in the facts and information make much more impact and lodge in the memory. The principle applies to our students, too, and it works both ways. It is well worth considering ways in which the medium of drama and performance might be used in our teaching to support the delivery of other topics. This isn't an innovation or new, but I would suggest that it's an area which gets overlooked. Why not ask other classroom teachers (or heads of department) of the year groups that you teach which topics the students are studying in their other lessons. These topics could well provide inspiration for topics or subjects that you could cover in your drama lessons with them or be used to explore different drama strategies and performance techniques. It's always good for us, as teachers, to break out of our drama 'bubble' occasionally and see what our colleagues in other areas are doing. Not only is this good for developing professional relationships in school but it gives us some unofficial CPD. We can reflect on how we might be more creative (that word again) in our own teaching. We can refresh the content we deliver and implement different ways in which this content can be delivered. Similarly, colleagues in other subjects might be grateful for our specialized experience in helping them deliver their own content.

Some of the best and most innovative teaching I've seen or taken part in is when genuine cross-curricular links have been made and are carefully coordinated and developed. As part of my work in a partner school, I remember watching a Geography lesson which was, to my eyes, almost indistinguishable from a drama lesson. The students were learning about the Aberfan disaster, where a colliery spoil tip on a slope of mountain collapsed and landed on the village of Aberfan. The disaster claimed the lives of 144 people, 116 of whom were children. I was, frankly, in awe of the Geography teacher who was skilfully using verbatim theatre techniques and docudrama to examine the physical and geographical circumstances of the disaster, as well as the human and emotional impact. Students were retaining all of the key information about the disaster and were able to discuss it in real detail. The emotional and human angle, I would argue, was their way in. Some of the work the students produced was genuinely moving. Perhaps more impressively, the impact on the students was instantly visible. They were learning about geography (and much more besides) through drama techniques. Two for the price of one, if you're inclined to measure these things numerically. I'm not. In my own teaching career, a genuine highlight was a collaborative project that I worked on with colleagues from English, History, Religious Studies and Music. To celebrate the centenary of the end of the First

World War, we wanted to create something which reflected on the war through the lens of our own school. We were fortunate to have a well-preserved archive of material from this period, and we worked together, each bringing our different skills to the table, to develop something to mark this occasion. That 'something' turned out to be an interactive piece of performance using music, song, images, poetry, prose and historical artefacts to look at the impact of the First World War on our own school community. This performance was staged several times throughout one day to mark the centenary, so that all students and members of staff could see it, and then capped off with an evening performance for parents. I learned an enormous amount about my colleagues and their skills in their own subjects. At the same time, I was able to use my own skills to help bring all of the different threads together and stage something which was easily understood by an audience of all ages and 'worked' as a performance. The finished piece itself, largely down to the skill and brilliance of the student performers, was indescribably moving. To describe the finished product as a success (or even a product) might seem crass, but it made a huge impact on the school community and is fondly remembered. Not that I wasn't convinced or needed to be persuaded, but genuine collaborative work with other subject specialists was a real eye-opener for me. And who felt the benefit of this approach the most? The students.

Working with senior leadership teams

You might read the words in that subheading and sigh. Or harrumph. And wonder if there's ever any way of keeping SLT happy. Take a deep breath, adopt a calming yoga position (if that helps) and try to park any cynicism that you might have for just a moment.

I have worked with genuinely inspiring and brilliant members of senior leadership teams. It's fair to say that I've also worked for some senior leaders who were unreliable, inconsistent and didn't always have the best interests of students (or staff) at heart. We deserve the former and need them to be able to do our job properly, but we sometimes get the latter. I don't propose to provide suggestions or ideas for how to deal with the latter, other than some fantastically baroque swearing in isolation in your car on the way home from work. My focus here is to think about what we need from our senior leaders, and how we can work with them so that they provide us with the support and flexibility that we need, whilst ensuring that they have a real understanding of our subject and why it sometimes doesn't fit neatly into predefined whole-school models. Our students' work is uniquely collaborative and a mixture of practical, theory and writing. It should be taught in bespoke and appropriate spaces. Senior leaders, at the very least, need to make sure that we and our students have access to these spaces, as well as the resources within them, so that we can do our job properly. This works both ways, of course. If we want senior leaders to understand our subject and lend additional support, we have to deliver the goods as subject teachers.

Here's a point worth considering, which I mention because I never hear it mentioned in schools or initial teacher training. As teachers, just as in any other employment sector, our contracts outline our duties and responsibilities, our terms of employment and the hours we are expected to work. We are, therefore, paid according to these terms. The bit I never hear teachers discussing (or very rarely, outside of trade union meetings) is stopping work at the end of the working day, or saying that they can't do things because it falls outside their contracted duties. The amount of extra and often unpaid work done by teachers in schools, day in and day out, is extraordinary. By which, I mean that if you are marking work at home in an evening or weekend then you are undertaking unpaid work. Of course, a school can argue that marking the work is part of the duties and responsibilities associated with your contract. Yes, it absolutely is. But the workload has to be reasonable and, most importantly, *achievable* in the time you have available. It is too often the case that schools rely on the vocational dedication of their staff to do work for which they aren't properly or fairly remunerated. If you direct or help out with a school production, or any other extra-curricular activity, then this is on a voluntary basis. Most teachers willingly take this on and enjoy it, stressful as it can often be. Without wanting to sound too 'out, brothers, out', we must bear in mind that if we are showing this level of willing, where we are often undertaking unpaid work or making a voluntary contribution to the broader corporate life of the school, we expect that this should be duly recognized by senior leaders, and appreciated.

I work in a school and it's probably the case that if I was currently working with terrible senior leaders, I would still say (in writing, in this book, which there is every chance they might read) that they are brilliant and supportive. Let me say, then, that I am fully aware of how lucky I am that my current senior leadership team is incredibly supportive. Not just of me as an individual but of my departmental colleagues, and the subject itself. We are generously resourced and appropriately staffed. We are also given relative freedom to shape and innovate within the curriculum as we see fit. As a result, the students have a great experience in our subject, whether this is in curriculum lessons or as part of our extra-curricular provision. The most important point here is that I used the word 'lucky' to describe my situation, and I shouldn't have to. This situation should be typical, de rigueur, and happening in every school up and down the country.

We are only able to do our jobs well, we are only able to be better than merely satisfactory, when we have the meaningful support and understanding of our senior leaders. It is all too rare that our own senior leaders come from a performing arts background themselves. You might be one of the lucky ones who has a senior leader with that sort of teaching experience and an inherent understanding of your subject. More often than not, though, we need to explain the specifics of our subject with senior managers who don't have a background or experience in what we do. In an ideal world, good senior leadership involves trust. That trust means that, as subject specialists, we are empowered to make decisions about the curriculum we deliver, the exam boards we choose and how we structure our curriculum and assessment within it. Obviously, we also need to fall in line and meet requirements which apply to the whole school – reporting, parents' evenings, teacher training days and so on.

The reality is about understanding that a degree of subtle negotiation is involved. Why, for instance, would any of us be inclined to carry out hours of additional work on a school production if we are routinely not given the resources and facilities to deliver the curriculum properly in our classroom teaching? The collective goodwill of drama teachers is astonishing. Social media groups dedicated to drama teaching are a daily testament to the 'above and beyond' work that is done every single day in schools, including weekends! So much is done in the name of doing everything possible to help and support the students that we teach. Make sure you are willing to do your bit for your school community, providing that your school leadership is being fair and supportive and flexible with you. A failure to demand proper support from your senior leaders can (not will but *can*) pave the way for problems and tensions down the line. Remember your guiding principles, your core values, and stick with them.

The school production

I write about this as though it's singular, but for many of us it is the case that we are involved with all sorts of extra-curricular production work throughout the academic year. This might also be on top of showcasing curriculum work for parents and the school community. Frankly, I've never known a school production which *wasn't* stressful. They are also one of the highlights of some pupils' entire school careers, and it's often the case that when actors are interviewed about their work and their starting point with all things thespian, they cite that first school production they took part in. Some schools tackle an enormous production annually, whilst others do them every other year. It might be the case that your school tackles a musical and a play each year, for example. Schools with internal house systems might also mount house plays. A great number of schools also enter groups into the annual Schools' Shakespeare Festival, which is offered by the Shakespeare Schools Foundation. Other schools take part in the National Theatre's *Connections* project, at either a local or a national level. All of this takes a huge amount of time, of course, and it's relatively rare that students can be taken off timetable to make a production happen. School productions rely on time after school and sometimes at weekends to complete rehearsals. None of this is without stress and is a frequent source of anxiety for the teachers involved. There are ways of minimizing the stress associated with the productions you take work on, however.

Firstly, make sure that the production you choose is both something that's going to provide meaningful and exciting opportunities for students (and not just as performers, but backstage and as technicians and wardrobe, prop and front-of-house 'staff' also) and also something that you – or whoever is directing it – really enjoys. These productions tend to become something of a labour of love; if you love what it is, that passion is more likely to be communicated to the students in the company and create something which is successful. It should be a statement of the obvious but you will need an appropriate budget which will have a degree of flexibility and cover any performance rights for the show, as well as the materials for set, costume, props and anything else that's needed. I say it should be a statement of the obvious, but I am still shocked that there are headteachers asking drama specialists to direct and stage a school production with *no budget*. Please, for the sake of your sanity and well-being, if you ever find yourself in this position do not agree to it. You might need an agreement with your school about a budget for the production and what happens to any proceeds from ticket sales, but you *will* need a budget. I have seen confident and capable teachers reduced to tears because they don't have a budget, or they aren't allowed proper rehearsal time, or adequate resources. And this might be before you've done a moment's rehearsal.

The best school productions are the ones I've seen where budgets are clearly somewhat limited, but the stage is full of students evidently having a great time, and a real sense of community, of the school joining up to support the work. A school near me regularly stages ambitious musicals with a cast of around 100. What they may lack for in budget for set and razzamatazz, they more than make up for in attention to detail, talent and wit. Even more impressive is the platoon of teachers helping to sell tickets and programmes, organizing the raffle and selling drinks and refreshments at the interval. This is in addition, of course, to the teachers who have directed and staged the show as well as those frantically marshalling students backstage. Ask for help if you're directing a school production. You might need to call in some favours from your colleagues. Don't be shy – do it.

If you've agreed to direct a production (or even be a part of a production team which needs you to use your skills set and experience), then an essential requirement is that you publish a rehearsal schedule and circulate this to the cast and their parents at the audition stage. Treat it as a sacred written contract if you need to. Students will forget dental appointments, family birthdays, pets' birthdays, sports fixtures, detentions and all manner of things. Trying to get a cast and company together for regular rehearsals, especially at the end of a school day, can be a challenge. Students will need reminding and coaxing and this can become stressful in itself. Don't go it alone; lean on your colleagues and ask them to take on some responsibilities throughout the process. If you are in the fortunate position of having any on-site technical support or theatre technicians, then count your blessings and be sure to make them cups of tea and smile at them. Should you not be so lucky, you will need to set aside time for technical rehearsals, as well as finding suitably skilled people to help with the technical aspects of your production. Be sure to seek these people out and get a firm commitment from them well in advance. Colleagues from all over the school might well surprise you in terms of their willingness to help and their theatrical experience. It isn't just the Art department, for example, who can paint the set and design your publicity poster and programme. There is sometimes enough talent within the cast and company to be able to take on these responsibilities.

You don't need to see yourself as a West End impresario and certainly don't need to behave like one. I once worked with a colleague who was given financial carte blanche when staging a production of their favourite, cherished musical. I'll cut to the chase. This colleague spent £37,000 on that production. You read that correctly. This was for a school production of a musical with a cast of forty. To give some sense of comparison, this was at a time when a teacher's starting salary was only slightly higher than half that amount. The audience loved it and so did the students performing in it; but what message did it send about theatrical endeavour? That production budget figure was announced as something of a triumph to anyone who would listen. The audience would have loved a production of the same musical staged for a fraction of that exorbitant sum, providing that it was ambitious, creative, well sung and entertaining. Similarly, the cast would still have had the time of their lives whether there was automated moving scenery (I promise this actually happened) or not. Some staff were disappointed that this was allowed to happen, and with other extra-curricular productions given a tiny fraction of that amount, it created division and jealousy between students and some staff. We work on school productions to enrich, to create opportunity and to give students an experience of performance that they can't get through curricular drama lessons. That is noble enough in itself. We don't need to look in the mirror and think that we are seeing Cameron Mackintosh staring back at us.

Finally, don't forget that these productions are truly valuable. Again, I'm not measuring this in the numerical or fiscal sense, but certainly in how they can inspire and provoke a love of performing and performance. Students can develop their skills in our subject in so many ways in a school production which can't be tackled in the day-to-day curriculum. One will enrich and benefit the other. In the same way, the school community benefits, too. A production, a performance, brings people from all strands of the school together. Parents, governors, non-teaching staff, students, colleagues. Our working days can be busy and stressful, but a school performance should be uplifting and celebratory. Finally, *we* benefit enormously as professionals. Directing or producing school productions looks great on CVs and résumés and shows that we can plan, manage, coordinate and work with budgets. Successful productions show that we are willing to go 'above and beyond' and also provide a much-needed shop window for our subject. Yes, they can be stressful, but you can put things is place along the way to help manage that stress.

'We've had the call!'

Whilst sort of paraphrasing the marvellous Annie Potts in the first *Ghostbusters* movie, for teachers everywhere, these words can create instant fear, panic, dread and stress. You know what those words mean. Ofsted has made the phone call to school and notified them that the inspection is imminent. SOUND THE ALARMS! Or, rather, try not to. Before we look at how to cope with the imminent arrival of Ofsted inspectors (I know that independent schools use ISI [Independent Schools' Inspectorate] but the system remains broadly the same, and I'll refer to them here as Ofsted as majority rules), it's worth remembering that it's really easy to be prepared and successfully demonstrate how brilliant you are at what you do *if* you're systematic about collating and recording relevant evidence and information on a semi-regular basis. If this isn't how you work, then prepare for forty-eight hours of some fairly frenzied flapping and worrying. I'm not trying to downplay how inherently stressful any sort of inspection is going to be. There will absolutely be some amount of unavoidable stress; being placed under scrutiny, whether it's directly as the smile-free zone that is the Ofsted inspector tiptoes into the start of your lesson or remotely as your department is given the once over, someone is making a judgement about what it is that we do and how well we do it. Best, then, to think about ways to minimize the impact of the stress associated with an inspection and consider how we might best go about being properly prepared for being scrutinized.

It's almost inevitable that between the time of writing and the time of publication, this book will be dated in terms of what it is that Ofsted wants to see when they visit. One of the government's most high-profile non-ministerial departments, its staff and policies still come under enormous pressure from politicians and ministers of all stripes, as well as keen media interest. During my time in the profession, 'what Ofsted will be looking for' has changed time and time again. Currently, this season's Ofsted fashion trends would seem to be 'deep dives' into specific curriculum areas, rather than the whole school, and a focus on how much 'impact' teachers make. Whilst it's entirely reasonable to anticipate that this focus will change the next time there's a cabinet reshuffle or senior Ofsted resignation, what remains constant is Ofsted making some sort of judgement or decision about the quality of education that our school provides. This might mean making a direct judgement on your teaching or on our beloved subject area. I'm always worried that Ofsted inspectors won't fundamentally 'get' what it is that we do in drama. Convinced that a long-retired scientist will end up scowling in the corner of my studio during a boisterous practical devising session, I used to be inclined to think up ways to keep demonstrating that my students were unmistakably *learning*. This nightmare scenario has never actually presented itself and I've never had a bad experience with Ofsted inspectors themselves. My worst experiences surrounding inspections have been where senior management have made panicky knee-jerk reactions to the imminent inspection and created an enormous administrative workload for staff, as well as enabling a climate of fear and dread. If this happens, make your office or workspace your sanctuary. Though the mugs and tea towels are unbearably smug, at this stage there really is something to be said for *Keep calm and carry on.* By just cracking on and doing what we do well, and ensuring that we are rigorous, systematic and capture evidence of what we do, the students can carry on learning and not much should change for an inspection. Through this everyday learning, Ofsted inspectors can then make a judgement about how good we are, or about the quality of teaching and/or learning that is taking place. Dressing it up with bells and whistles is pointless; if the students are in the middle of a practical devising project, then that is what that lesson should focus on. Resist the calls of any senior managers who tell you that this lesson must now become 'a theory lesson' (they're learning about dramatic theories through their practical work in any rehearsal or devising process) or a 'chalk and talk' lesson. You and your students will be more relaxed if you just carry on as normal.

It comes back to the importance of advanced planning and then ensuring that there is a system in place to capture and record evidence, whatever form that evidence might take. It's fair to say that the capturing of evidence in our subject area might require a little more thought than some other subjects, so we need to be systematic in our approach. At the start of the academic year, you might well have some sort of internal data compliance tasks at your school; overviews of schemes of work, lesson plans, assessment points, departmental mark schemes and handbooks. Better to devote the thinking and planning time to it in September (when you might, with any luck, be refreshed after a couple of weeks on a beach or in your back garden) than under pressure and surrounded by panic when 'the call' comes in. If you're working in a department where you're not a lone ranger, divide up the tasks and have corporate responsibility for ensuring that paperwork is in place. As the academic year gets underway and teaching gets into full swing, remember the points earlier (in Chapter 2) in this book about creating your own assessment models and strategies and making them work for you and your students. Mark books with evidence of your observations or practical sessions and class performances are useful. Filmed performance of some class work is another excellent way of demonstrating learning and assessment, often in lieu of a regular exercise book. I now insist that my students submit written work electronically. This means that there is a record – for them and for me – of when it was submitted, that I can archive it and then easily write comments and suggestions on it with proposed feedback or areas for improvement. Archiving these on a computer in clearly labelled folders during the course of the year's teaching is truly the work of moments and will avoid a mad scramble through your 'deleted items' folder or the mountain of rogue paperwork on your desk. We can absolutely ensure that there is ample evidence of learning taking place and that it is well-structured, clear and demonstrative of meaningful assessment. But to do this successfully and sidestep some of the stress that Ofsted brings, we need to make the effort as we go; little and often.

In addition to what we do as part of our curriculum, remember to keep a note of everything extra that you (and your department) do throughout the year; again, do it as you go, and whilst you remember. Booked a school trip to see *The Woman In Black*? Write it down. Helped someone with an audition speech for drama school? Get it on the list. Directed a school production with a cast of sixty and a backstage crew of twenty? Ofsted want to know about things like this, so make a record of it and make sure that you find a way to let them know how much you do if they end up in your lesson. Think about their presence as being a great opportunity to show off the work done in class (they're looking for good practice) and an opportunity for you to be a great ambassador for the subject and take pride in all the extra that goes on. Our subject, by its very nature, generates lots of 'extra', and though this might vary from year to year, it isn't hard to show how many students have benefited from drama and the opportunities that our subject creates. If you need to, spend an hour before Ofsted arrives making an eye-catching display in a corridor or studio which lists all of the statistics which go to prove just how great you are. From personal experience, and to the best of my knowledge, I've never been observed teaching by a drama specialist as part of an inspection. I was, though, observed teaching by a very understanding gentleman who was happy to pick up his piles of papers and brush himself down when two of my more rowdy Year 10 boys decided to create an impromptu fight sequence as part of a devising lesson looking at the Vietnam War. I mention this to remind you that even though the person watching you teach might not be a drama education specialist (as you are), they *are* human and understand students and how students behave. Or how students will misbehave. Keep your nerve and remember that it's finite and the inspection itself, including the 'pre-drinks' panic period, can and will only last for a few days. Write a list of everything that you have to do, which should including getting at least eight hours' sleep a night, and tick them off as you do them. Most importantly, remember that *you* are the subject specialist. *You* are the expert where drama is concerned here. Senior managers might arrive red-faced and panicked and making untimely demands, but as long as all of your data and paperwork is compliant, accurate, organized and accessible, then you have nothing to worry about. When I worked in a different establishment, I remember 'the call' arriving and a senior leader trying to hastily implement an entirely new system of 'gold standard folders' and have this up and running in forty-eight hours. It fell flat on its face, of course. You can't create and implement a brand-new system in two days' time whilst preparing for inspection. The reason that some senior managers (and it's some, not all) stress or become unnecessarily innovative when inspection looms is because it's their metaphorical neck on the equally metaphorical block. So let them get on with proving that they are providing genuinely outstanding leadership and management, and remember to keep your focus on demonstrating, through your teaching and your collected data, that you are a brilliant drama teacher. (And have a really amazing treat waiting for you at home on the night that the inspection finishes. That's an order.)

The administrative burden

'*We are a proudly paperless college*', the member of staff told me with
evident sincerity and satisfaction, as we walked around the building
where I was being interviewed for a job, an exciting promotion. (I
didn't get it; it went to an internal candidate, but they did continue
to use the lesson plan I had brought for my lesson observation
with taster groups at open evenings the following academic year.)
And, everywhere I looked, paper. Paper, paper and more paper. On
noticeboards, piled up on windowsills and on desks. Bookcases with
paper cascading down them in every classroom. Students relying on
and carrying round with them – you guessed it – paper. Either the
member of staff didn't understand what the word 'paperless' actually
meant or they were willing to turn a blind eye to the amount of
pulped and processed rainforest that was on display wherever we
went. This was a neat illustration of the dichotomy that exists when
we come to think about administration. I'm fully aware that paper
doesn't necessarily equal administration, and that administration
can also involve much more than paper. But it's a good place to start
when we think about how much extra work we create for ourselves,
especially that which is unnecessary. Whether this is in extraneous
meetings (those meetings which seem to exist to only agree on the
next meetings), unnecessary emails cluttering your inbox or the piles
of paper which duplicate existing material, as teachers we can drown
in admin if we aren't careful. This is before we start to think about
the administrative workload that our subject brings; whether this is
tangible (physical, visible) or 'invisible', administration brings with it
stress. So often, so much of this administration and associated stress
can be minimized or avoided altogether. Institutions tend to generate
admin work; the bigger the institution, the greater the administrative

burden is likely to be. The steps that we can take to reduce the stress associated with administration often start with ourselves.

When I was training to be a teacher, the digital revolution which had really made an impact on homes and businesses at the end of the 1990s hadn't quite reached mainstream education. I vividly remember the awestruck gasps in the room when our PGCE tutor first showed us a – brace yourself – USB stick. Set to revolutionize our working lives in the way that the wheel or the microchip had done to previous generations, we were told that for the modest sum of around £20 this small device could probably just about hold a term's lesson plans and a scheme of work outline. We knew, surely, that the future had arrived, and it was so bright that shades weren't optional. Technological innovations are now so rapid that my own students genuinely didn't believe me when I recently told them that we used to have to pay every time we sent a text message. The advent of the USB, therefore, was going to make our working lives easier and, naturally, reduce all waste, excess paper and a significant administrative burden. I scarcely need to deliver the punchline which is that: it hasn't. If anything, the reverse is true. If anything, our working lives are more admin-drenched than they have ever been. In some respects, of course, the digital revolution has been unarguably brilliant in terms of supporting the work we do and our students' learning. One thing it hasn't done, though, is reduce or eliminate administration.

I've been on something of a personal crusade in my current school, or at least, within my department. Our office and teaching spaces were frequently covered in paper. Stray scripts, misplaced handouts and essential revision materials had become commonplace. My aim to try and move to becoming a genuinely paperless department didn't emerge from an environmentally friendly place, though this is another reason in itself to try to create less waste. I am firmly of the belief that our current mainstream educational system doesn't do enough to sincerely promote independent learning or create genuinely curious young people who are equipped with the skills to survive in higher education. Several generations of league tables, educational reforms and the political football-ing of our education system have meant that there is sometimes the leaning towards teaching only to the test, only delivering the content of the specification, and nothing further. As part of this, we are used to providing eye-catching PowerPoint presentations and physical handouts. Online forums for drama teachers are full of people politely asking (and sometimes pleading) for other people to share their resources. There is, I am convinced, an over-reliance on us providing physical handouts for our students which, in turn, creates rooms full of passive learners expecting to be spoon-fed the correct answers. Rather than having to directly engage with the content of the lesson, if students know that a handout is on the way, they can switch off, discreetly try and go on Snapchat without us noticing and silently commit to engage with the material later. The problem is that, all too often, this doesn't happen. Physical handouts don't always appear to have any value for students; they can end up in the bottom of bags, abandoned on studio floors or shoved in a folder. I made a resolve with my own exam-level groups that I would talk and let them create their own notes on a particular topic. Whilst I can use presentations to model exemplar responses, I want my students to make their own notes. This way, they stand more chance of them being coherent, individual and referred to later on. Yes, by doing this, there is a risk that the note-taking is poor or non-existent, but the onus is placed on the student to take responsibility for their own learning. In no way am I suggesting a return to mid-twentieth-century teaching, devoid of technology and relying on talking at a blackboard and throwing the blackboard eraser at students. But, despairing of generations of students who cannot effectively learn independently, there needs to be a balance between harnessing technology and making sure that students engage with our lessons. In the meantime, we can dramatically reduce the amount of administration and paperwork that we create. I do create resources for my students, but these days I am much more inclined to take sections of them and upload them to a central area instead of producing dozens of copies. Save the planet; reduce your stress levels.

There is, however, an unavoidable amount of administration associated with our jobs that we can't do much about. Short of ignoring some of our colleagues, we can't turn a blind eye to or switch off our emails. Reading emails takes up so much valuable time, and it's worth being willing to delete all the stuff that clogs up our inboxes so that we can focus on the jobs we really need to do. Starting with our classroom teaching, it's worth going through our resources and considering which might still work as successfully if they were digital or online resources instead of physical ones. A regular clearing out of inboxes, desks, shelves and studio spaces is also really valuable. In my experience, it can lead to questions such as, *How do students manage to leave the drama lesson with only one shoe on?* But it's worthwhile to keep your working life as free from clutter as possible. One area that is worth looking at, if only to be aware of its burden, is the administration associated with public exams in our subject.

Whilst I am aware of the amount of specialist work that goes into supporting public exams in Music and Art, the amount of administration – and time – that goes into facilitating successful exams in Drama is considerable. I touched on this in Chapter 3, but it is well worth considering that the organization of any exams which aren't set in traditional examination rooms is going to require you to be proactive with administration. Some boards are clearer than others about their expectations of you and what you need to do. Firstly, if you aren't sure or it isn't clear what you need to do, contact the exam board yourself, as far in advance as possible. Each exam (even though it might be classed as non-examination assessment) comes with strict guidance and paperwork which we need to adhere to as teachers. Again, these will vary from board to board but the constant is that we need to be proactive and well prepared. Students will need to sign candidate identification forms and sign and declare that the work is their own; we will typically need to countersign these. For exams of scripted performances, texts need to be bought, abridged, cast and directed. There needs to be regular contact with any visiting examiner, and performance schedules, running orders and students' own notes will need to be made available. When it comes to assessing devising work, we need to provide a justification and supporting commentary for our marking. A bonus, if you can call it that, is that we get to watch our own students as they 'sit the exam', when they perform. Personally, I find this a little bit of a nerve-shredder, praying that the examiner is fair-minded and gives the students the marks they are due. Even to get to that point though, drama teachers have effectively had to create and run the exam itself. If in any doubt, make yourself a checklist; a physical one. Tick things off as they are prepared and ready or as they are sent to the board. It's easy to feel a little overwhelmed when it comes to administrating drama exams, but being properly organized and understanding exactly what the requirements are is fundamental to helping to make this aspect of our working lives a little less stressful.

The lone rangers

My friend Jenny Moon was the first person of my own age who I knew who successfully trained to be a drama teacher. This was before I had even considered going into the profession. I remember phoning her to congratulate her on getting her first job. She was ecstatic; she was going to be – as an NQT – Head of Drama, a lone ranger, the sole teacher in charge of the subject in her secondary school. Even then, the thought of being the only teacher in a school with experience and understanding of that subject filled me with a sort of empathetic fear. Now, many years later, it fills me with nothing but admiration for the people who do this. I've never personally been in the position where I have been the only drama teacher in my place of work. I've found the subject knowledge, experience and camaraderie of my drama colleagues an essential part of my survival and development as a teacher. Arriving 'fresh off the boat' as an NQT into a busy sixth form college, it was my colleagues who mentored me, pointed me in the right direction and stopped me from dropping off the proverbial cliff edge as I was about to casually waltz into a scheme of work or topic which might be disastrous. Being qualified to teach, and by which I mean having achieved QTS as part of a teacher training programme, doesn't mean you can actually teach *well*. QTS, a bit like passing your driving test, means you are just about roadworthy in the classroom, if you don't mind the mixing of metaphors. You go on to learn how to teach properly and effectively through day-to-day classroom teaching and getting on with the job. Which is why I am constantly in awe of those of you in the profession who are the lone rangers; the sole teachers in charge of drama in your school. This responsibility and isolation can bring with it additional stress, though. But there are ways to acknowledge and minimize the impact of that stress.

I've been asked to work with lone rangers (let's go with that phrase) in schools in a supportive capacity over the years and the main issue they face is always lack of confidence. However supportive and engaged their leadership or line management might be, they don't often have the opportunity to float ideas, discuss possibilities and ask for advice and, thus, gain confidence in their subject and the delivery of it. In ever-decreasing circles, a lack of opportunity to ask questions or make comparisons with other colleagues often leads to a spiral of self-doubt and lack of confidence which is hard to crawl back from. Lone rangers need to make the effort to forge links beyond the walls of their school. There is help and support out there, but accessing it requires initiative. Firstly, whichever exam board you use can provide resources to support, whether they are online or physical. These might include sample schemes of work, past exam papers or additional resources which can support either the exam specification or teaching lower down the school. These are (usually) free and of high quality. Furthermore, but perhaps less well broadcast to schools, is exam boards' willingness to provide in-school support or training opportunities. Exam boards are in competition with one another and each one wants you to choose them. This is why they are often so willing to provide face-to-face support and training. Some of them even have bespoke (if discreet) budgets for this, so they're a good first port of call to find a lifeline. At least in this way, if you're a lone ranger you can feel like you're connected to *something*. Exam boards can also be really helpful and link you to other schools in your area that are delivering the same specifications. Whilst this might be initially about having a point of reference for the exam board content, this can create much-needed opportunities to be part of a relevant and local network. The exam board probably won't pick up the phone and offer you this; be proactive and drop them an email and ask for help.

Another way that lone rangers can feel a little less isolated is by forging links with any local theatres. Again, supporting schools is something which is usually within the remit of theatres. Any theatre company (whether they have a permanent physical base or not) which receives Arts Council funding will have to engage with their community and provide educational access as part of their funding remit. Resources are spread pretty thin and they aren't limitless, but lots of theatres run free networking events for teachers, workshops to support schools and students and heavily discounted tickets to productions. Get in touch with your local (professional) theatre and ask if there are any ways in which they can help. We are lucky that the majority of producing theatres will create free education packs to accompany their productions; this is becoming more and more common. These are usually well written and structured by someone with an understanding of what it is that teachers actually need. I've always found these packs especially useful in providing insight into the production process, which gives exemplification and illustration of the design process as part of the production.

If you're internally assessing work (performance work or written work where you have to mark it and then send it to the exam board for a check that it meets the agreed national standard), then this can be hard to do in isolation. Most exam boards provide clear guidance for teachers with relevant standardization materials and commentaries so that you can check that your marking is in line with expectations. When this standardization material isn't readily available, this standard can be hard to get a grip on, especially if there's no one around to talk it through with. What we all need when it comes to standardization is someone who can cast an eye over our marking and provide feedback; usually as part of a reciprocal process. If you're a lone ranger and struggling with this aspect of curriculum delivery, ask your senior leadership team to make enquiries with other schools that you're linked to. This might be as part of a multi-academy trust or a local area network, but there should be some sort of existing collective in place. You cannot (and should not) be expected to do this on your own and get it right all the time. Asking for help and additional support is in no way an admission of failure. It's the opposite, in fact; a demonstration that you're willing to go above and beyond to make sure that you meet the standard and that your students' work is accurately marked. Perhaps your school can arrange some time for you to go to (or to host) local colleagues and have a sharing of work between you. This will act as professional development in kind and should also leave you feeling more confident in your own abilities.

It might be the case that our own non-subject specialist colleagues can provide us with guidance and support. This is usually limited to help from a pedagogical perspective or with insight into the particularities of individual pupils. In my experience, it is rare that non-drama colleagues are able to provide much guidance by way of subject knowledge or in terms of curriculum delivery in our subject area. It is sometimes the case that schools might pad out an English teacher's timetable with some lessons teaching drama. There are even jobs which stipulate a combination of both subjects. This always perplexes me. Yes, both subjects have some focus on the teaching of play texts, but the ways that these plays are taught and explored are very different. How do schools think they can find effective delivery of both of these discrete subjects in one candidate? I'm not saying such candidates – such teachers – don't exist, but there can't be all that many of them. It often strikes me that the wish for a teacher of both English and drama is a financial decision rather than one which best serves the needs of the students. With the caveat that I have taught alongside some genuinely brilliant and talented teachers of English and drama (and it's always that way around, English being their first or dominant subject), it is more often the case that when English teachers are asked to teach drama, it doesn't always seem to work very well. I can't imagine it's much fun for the English teacher in this scenario either, but I find it striking that it is much more rarely the case that a drama teacher is asked to fill up gaps in their timetable with some English. Only a cynic would suggest that some schools inherently value English more than they value drama, and I don't want to come across as a cynic (he added, cynically). I wouldn't know where to start if it came to teaching a play text to students in an English lesson, and would probably make a complete hash of it. Better, then, to seek support from subject specialists, wherever they may be.

A final thought on the needs of the lone ranger. During the writing of this book, I was asked to go into a school in a fairly remote area and provide support to their drama teacher. As the emails pinged back and forth to set up the training day, I realized that something seemed a bit 'off' but I couldn't put my finger on it. When I arrived at the school, all became clear. The drama teacher was a lone ranger and had been brought into the school two years previously to introduce drama as a subject to the curriculum. The school itself had no extra-curricular tradition in performances or drama being taught at *any* level. This drama teacher had their work cut out. Having been bursting with energy and ideas in their previous role, this drama teacher had arrived at this school ready to take on the world and give the subject the big push it needed. Fast forward to my arrival and it was clear that the intervening two years had presented unforeseen challenges. The cohort of Year 11 students who made up the school's first ever GCSE drama class were behind in some areas and struggling to catch up. This was because the school's lone ranger drama teacher had been absent for long periods owing to a period of genuine personal tragedy and trauma. My heart ached for them. This teacher, on their own, in an office on a quiet corridor with no other colleagues nearby, was now expected to work miracles and get these students their GCSEs. In their absence, the school had not provided these students with any sort of specialist drama provision. And yet, the drama teacher felt that they were responsible. *'If these kids don't get their GCSE, it's completely my fault'*, the teacher said. Absolute nonsense. This was a situation where a school had not done anywhere near enough to support this teacher, plunged into difficult circumstances. Even more alarming was the fact that now that this teacher was back in school, there didn't seem to be anything in place in the way of support for them, or their students. My day with this teacher was an education for us both. I did my best to create strategies to help this teacher get their students through the GCSE course and make some concrete plans for the next academic year. At the same time, I learned about the value of real and tangible support from our places of work. Without it, we are going to struggle and might, worst-case scenario, fail. If we are a lone ranger, without appropriate help and support, we are almost certainly on a trajectory to failure. My heart ached because this drama teacher – and I hope they are reading this – was evidently *brilliant*; dynamic, energetic, passionate about their subject, bang up to date with subject knowledge and working overtime to support their students. What they lacked was confidence and support. Confidence doesn't happen overnight; it comes over time. Support, however, can be put in place relatively quickly and can make life easier. If you are struggling, especially if you are a lone ranger, make sure you are receiving adequate and appropriate support. It is in no way too much to ask for. Your employer owes it to you.

Non-subject specialists

Finally, it's worth a quick look at how non-subject specialists might cope when delivering our subject. Having briefly touched on this when thinking about the English and drama crossover points, it's also worth thinking about what support and resources should be available for those who have found themselves asked to deliver drama when they don't have any background in it. I'm not sure that this is in any way an ideal scenario for anyone concerned, student or teacher, but sometimes these situations will arise. Social media groups often receive a heartfelt and desperate plea from the teacher asking for help in how they might deliver a subject in which they have no background or training. Quite. There is no easy solution to this problem. The most straightforward way to cope is to revert to the coat/hanger dilemma (from Chapter 1) and for you to use your own subject as the medium through which to deliver drama skills. If you're not an expert in drama, then you're going to have to rely on what you *are* good at, and that's likely to be your own subject area. Depending on where the students are in their journey through the school, they will have acquired some knowledge of drama skills and devices and should be able to apply them. Some sort of baseline assessment will help you to see what the students are good at and what they aren't good at. You might be able to see where the gaps in their learning are. If you're really unlucky (presumably wicked in a past life level of unlucky), then you might have to teach a subject that you're not trained in to students at GCSE and A level. However enthusiastic you might be, it really is short-changing the students in these critical exam phases of their education. Schools shouldn't be asking non-subject specialists to deliver curriculum at this level (or at any level, frankly) and you would have every right to say no. This might mean turning down work and you're in no financial position to do so. I can empathize; I've been there and it sucks. If you are required to deliver an exam specification, though, it's time to invest in some drama textbooks which support the subject. Time to crack out that highlighter and start planning lessons from the textbook. Use the specification to work out what the endpoint requirements are and work backwards from there.

Remember my mentioning of drama teachers having occasional pockets of deep, specialized knowledge about odd things? In the same way, non-subject specialists will also probably have some knowledge of how drama works. There aren't many people who haven't seen a film or a play or a TV show. Most people have their favourite actors and their favourite performances. Even better: most people have an opinion about these actors and their performances. They've watched them act and reached a verdict about them and what they do. On some level, they have analysed and evaluated these actors' skills and their abilities. Think about what it is about your favourite performers that makes them appeal to you. Read reviews of their acting; well-written reviews will often discuss performances (and drama more generally) using technical language as part of its vocabulary. Roger Ebert's or Pauline Kael's film reviews are legendary for a reason. They both manage to use their writing to home in on why drama works, albeit in film. They discuss genre, style, scripts, storytelling and the technicalities of what actors do on a regular basis. In the theatre, the critical writings of Susannah Clapp, Arifa Akbar and Matt Trueman are routinely laser-sharp in their 'reading' of a live performance and helping the reader to understand how the performances and different design elements coalesce to create the live experience. Critical reviews offer astute analysis and an evaluative judgement. They share common ground with the GCSE and A level drama student and the non-subject specialist.

Finally, the best way to feel a little less stressed if you're slung into this sort of situation is to slowly grow your confidence. If you can teach, you can teach. The pedagogical theory remains constant between subjects, but what you're lacking is experience and confidence in the subject itself. Why not try and gain some? Go to the theatre, if you possibly can. If it's Shakespeare and it's a comedy, you'll be able to spot the English teachers because they'll be the ones laughing at the tiresome jokes about beards and syphilis. It might be a Harold Pinter play with pauses you could herd sheep through and start to wonder whether the actors have forgotten their lines. Maybe it's a Stephen Sondheim musical where there will be some melodies, but you'll have to do some heavy listening to be able to spot them. Yes, this is a glib take on three undisputed theatrical greats, but you can only really gain an understanding of what they do and why they work by going to see them in performance. Reading *Othello* or *The Birthday Party* or listening to *Follies* and *Into the Woods* is pleasant enough, but won't help you understand how drama works in performance. And there is a difference between drama and performance. Which leads us neatly on to how we can keep our subject knowledge relevant and refreshed.

5

Engaging with contemporary work

This part of the book might make you wince a little bit. As drama education practitioners we have a duty (yes, a duty) to engage directly with the development of our subject, both in the pedagogical and in the theatrical sense. I don't propose to suggest how you might engage with the pedagogical developments of this or any subject; this isn't that sort of book. Also, by the time I have committed the words to the page, a new initiative or educational innovation will be in place, and what I've written will be out of date. If you're looking to stay abreast of developments in drama education, then offering to mentor or support trainee teachers as part of a PGCE or initial teacher training course is a sound place to start. Besides which, the really good ones (and I say, without exaggeration, that my own teaching career has been enriched significantly by the brilliant trainees I have mentored over the years) come into your department full of energy and bursting with new ideas and things to try. And you can borrow these ideas. That's right: borrow. More importantly, though, we need to be aware that what we teach, whether it's core practical skills to our youngest students or ways of engaging with sometimes radical and left-of-centre contemporary theatre-going with our oldest students, we are umbilically linked to an art form as well as the teaching profession. Neither of these is at a standstill; the constant development and evolution of both means that the best drama teachers are those who are willing to engage with the subject as an art form and try and reflect it in their teaching. I'm not suggesting that simply because Katie Mitchell has, let's say, started to revolutionize video design that you have to try to bring this into your Year 8 lessons on a Friday afternoon. More often than I would like, though, when talking to drama teachers (wince alert) I'm shocked at how often they are willing to stick with the same-old, same-old, the dated or the dull. We all of us want to have a working life which doesn't overwhelm us with stress and is also going to be successful in terms of the outcomes for our students. What I'm suggesting is that we should be thinking about how we are defining that success. Assessments and exam results? Sure. Headteachers and school governors love those and we need to have a clear grip on them as previously discussed. Beyond that, though, there is so much scope for us to think about challenging our students whilst engaging them. Thinking about what sort of students we want to 'create'. Yes, there is a degree of risk-taking involved in this, but these risks can be calculated and considered so that, on balance, they are risks worth taking for the benefit of our students.

Staying relevant

When I sat one of the written papers as part of my A level in Theatre Studies, right at the end of the last millennium (Manchester United were about to win the treble and Geri Halliwell had just launched her solo career), I was confronted by the dreaded unseen extract. We had covered these in lessons and countless mock exams and practice papers, but it was always the trickiest part of the three (three!) written exams that were part of the qualification. The exam board could potentially throw *anything* at you – Greek tragedy, Restoration comedy, Noël Coward, Caryl Churchill – and the clock was ticking as you'd frantically read this unfamiliar extract and try and work out how this boy had turned into a giant dung beetle or why this recruitment consultant had invited all these different women from history to a celebratory dinner. In my exam, the board gave us an extract of Olwen Wymark's much-admired play *Find Me*. It focuses on Verity Taylor, a girl who is committed to a psychiatric unit where she sets fire to a chair. Written in 1977, its popularity has certainly endured with drama teachers, though it is rarely produced by professional theatres. Its most interesting dramatic device is that the role of Verity is, at various times, split into different facets of her personality: Verity One, Verity Two and so forth. I saw why the exam board was giving us this play and did my best to write about the possibilities of staging and directing this extract. *Find Me* is a well-written play. It provides challenges for performers, designers and directors. From a performance point of view, it offers a really meaty role to the actors who play any aspect of Verity. What surprises me enormously is that, given the wealth of exceptional new writing and theatrical innovation of the last twenty years or so, never mind the forty-plus years since the play was written, *Find Me* is still incredibly popular with drama teachers. It's impossible to say how popular, but for around ten years, every single year, without exaggeration, I would see performances of *Find Me* when I was examining performance work in schools. No matter whether it was GCSE or A level, or which schools and colleges I might be visiting, the length and breadth of the country, I would watch Verity's story unfold again and again. *Find Me* isn't the only play I'd see year after year. And I must stress that there is absolutely nothing *wrong* with the play. Occasionally, and it was only occasionally, it seemed to be a well-chosen play for the students who were performing in it. Most of the time, though, it seemed to have been chosen for its familiarity, for its relative ease for whoever had to direct it. The best drama teachers are those who try to engage with professional theatre practice; they are always learning. The alternative, whereby we reach for the same play again and again, year after year, regardless of the cohort, isn't likely to lead to an inspirational outcome. Students are not house bricks. Each cohort and every individual student in it needs to be considered on their own merits. And there will never be a mathematically perfect fit to get all those students into those plays. But it's a sure-fire route to ever-diminishing returns to keep reaching for the same play every single year. This is a plea to drama teachers everywhere – me included – do not just fall back on the texts which have brought former glories for you and your students. Resist the urge. If you had great results (however you might be looking to quantify those results) with a play, it was the unique combination of text, extract, casting, the examiner and the environment and circumstances of the performance itself. That one-off can never be recreated. We should always try to be looking forwards rather than backwards.

At the risk of sounding sanctimonious, I've reached for the tried-and-tested before now, and sometimes find myself doing it when I'm struggling to accommodate the whims and moods of my more challenging groups. A GCSE cohort will need to be divided into working groups and there are so many things to consider. The working dynamics of students (*I can't put him with her – they'll kill each other*), the amount of stage time each role has, how cunningly I might be able to try and hide a weaker student in a smaller role which is as close to their own type as possible. I've learned the hard way that trying to return to the successful texts of the past can bring problems and disappointments. When the exam boards were working with Ofqual to reform the subject at GCSE and A level, I was working in schools but also meeting and consulting with lots of teachers across the country to make sure that the end product was something which teachers would want to deliver. Sometimes, this was in a formal capacity, to see what they thought of the exam boards' latest proposals, and sometimes it was as part of a more informal networking event. I distinctly remember going to one such event and a head of a drama department pulling me to one side at the end of it. She was retiring, she told me, so any changes would make no impact on her working life, but she wanted to urge me to do something which would re-energize fatigued drama teachers and inspire their students at GCSE. '*Bring back Blue Remembered Hills*,' she told me, with a very sombre look on her face and the seriousness of a driving test examiner. I made some polite noises about the fact that all plays were up for discussion as potential set texts but shuddered internally and pondered this suggestion on the drive home. If you don't know it, Dennis Potter's *Blue Remembered Hills* was written as a play for television in 1979 and focuses on a group of seven-year-olds as they romp through the fields of their village, with the Second World War raging in the background. The television film's popularity is largely down to the striking performances of Helen Mirren, Michael Elphick and Janine Duvitski, as well as the central dramatic device in that these adult actors are playing seven-year-old children. Whether you find this entirely charming or so teeth-grindingly embarrassing that you can hardly look at the screen (I'll let you work out where I sit with this one), the play itself is fine, but certainly isn't the holy grail of all plays, the one to revitalize a subject in reform. The play had previously had a life as a set text with some exam boards and I was always baffled by this choice, just as I am when students perform extracts from it now. By giving the play's child roles to teenage students, the most intriguing dramatic device of the play itself is gone. The roles aren't being played by adults anymore – and Dennis Potter's rationale behind this dramatic device could scarcely be clearer – and, if it's a challenge for trained actors to manage these roles, it's even more problematic for young students. What typically emerges when GCSE students have a crack at *Blue Remembered Hills* is a generalized and stereotypical version of young children at play, without real detail or much believability. Furthermore, to bring back a former set text which had been abandoned once before would surely strike of (small c) conservative choices being made. What I was certain of then, and am even more certain of now, is that as drama teachers we have to try our very best to go forwards and not backwards. Of course, this doesn't mean discarding a wealth of dramatic texts just because they are from the past. But it does mean trying to strike a balance between delivering the canon (something that exam boards will always make a requirement) and recognizing that there are new, brilliant and exciting plays being written all the time. If you're ever looking to genuinely fire your students' creative impulses and help them to successfully engage with their practical work, I am convinced that there are plays which are more likely to do this than Dennis Potter's snapshot of the Forest of Dean.

Recently, I asked some of my A level students to bring in some music possibilities to help with their devising project. I'm always worried that my own choices will seem horribly dated or won't engage my students and think that they are bound to know music that I don't, and vice versa. One student arrived to the lesson and with wide-eyed excitement told me he had found a CD (remember those?) at home which belonged to his parents and he thought that the words of the songs were like poetry, genuinely profound and could help with their fledgling devised piece. '*I don't think you'll have heard of it, sir*', he said, firing up the album on Spotify on his phone, as the first notes of *Jagged Little Pill* started to play. Alanis Morissette's 1995 album has sold 33 million copies. Not only is it one of the bestselling albums of all time but it is also very familiar to anyone of my generation. It formed part of the soundtrack to our teenage years; I know every single word of it and think it holds up pretty well twenty-five years later. What was most striking was that none of my students had heard of it, or heard of Alanis Morissette herself. And why should they? They were familiar with a couple of tracks from their inclusion in films or on trailers for films and agreed that the words were 'deep'. The point that I'm making here is that, whilst we inevitably age, our students stay the same age. Each GCSE group, for example, thinks that their idea about using a pulsing red light to represent danger (or is it just my students?) is original and exciting. Every A level group thinks that by using the structure of TV shows and adverts, or by setting the piece in a psychiatric institution, they are being innovative. On our terms, of course, they're not. They're not being innovative or original. We've seen it a few hundred times before. But on *their* terms, the work they create is original, bold and full of dramatic potential. We must be careful to help nurture and develop this potential whilst also helping students to avoid hoary old dramatic clichés. A good way to try and stay relevant is to fuse the two sets of knowledge which are typically quite disparate; get your students to bring in things that they know, that are familiar to them and that interest them. We need to listen to our students and understand who they are, as individuals and as a group. At the same time, we are the professionals and will have more experience, and we need to bring this experience, together with the things that we know, to the table. I've stopped being shocked that some of my students have never watched *The Godfather* or *Don't Look Now* and have only just discovered *Friends* for the first time (most of them weren't even born when it finished) and remind myself that I'm equally unfamiliar with most of the things that they know and love. And that this situation is always likely to be the norm. A really easy and healthy way of staying relevant, then, is to make sure that we resist the urges to look back, rather than forwards, and to involve our students and their interests in their learning.

Theatre-going – no excuses

Another way to stay relevant and meaningfully engage with theatre and its developments is to actually – deep breath – go to the theatre itself. Let me assure you that I live in the same world that you do. The world where when a friend cancels plans on a weekday evening you're secretly delighted because you're exhausted, and can either lie on the sofa watching old episodes of *The Chase* on Challenge TV or – more than likely – stay a bit later after work and try and tackle that pile of coursework essays which are winking at you from the corner of your desk. It's the same world where parents' evenings, meetings, school production rehearsals, exam group 'extra lessons' and all sorts of family commitments can bring the ceiling down a little bit lower on most days. Those weeks where we turn a page in our diary, even if it's an electronic one, and see that we have 'stuff' on most days? Aren't most weeks like that? With the holidays that we get mostly reserved for catching up on sleep, cleaning out the terrifying vegetable drawer in the fridge or fending off the dreaded cold and flu which has been chasing us all half-term. Anyone else sick of people who aren't teachers saying, '*You teachers. All the holidays you get*'? Me too. I don't want to endorse violence here, so we need to think of an agreeable and peaceful way to respond to statements like that. Our holidays are paid annual leave and they are our sacred time. I mention all this because, whenever I suggest going to the theatre, teachers always tell me that they simply don't have time. Snap. Quite frankly, though, if we don't go to the theatre other than the theatre trips we have to run as part of the curriculum, there is no way that we can properly engage with the theatre and its developments as an art form. It is much easier said than done for me to say, '*Just go to the theatre*'. If we do that, then we might miss an evening of lying on the sofa and scrolling through Twitter and Instagram. Joking aside, it really should be an essential part of our jobs rather than a maybe. It's not just us teachers. I was once alarmed when I spoke with someone who was in a senior role which involved drama at one of the main exam boards and they proudly told me that they never went to the theatre. Ever. Amateur or professional. '*I see enough theatre being an examiner and watching practical work*', they said. I was speechless. Whilst it isn't a formal requirement of our profession that we make an effort to keep up with theatre-going, it is the case that we absolutely should. It's good for us and it's even better for our students. By maintaining an active interest in theatre itself, we stand the best chance of keeping our teaching practice and subject knowledge up to date and also finding things which will make our teaching – and our students' experience – better and richer.

Firstly, let me throw a potential cat amongst the proverbial pigeons. Does your school pay for you or your drama colleagues to go to the theatre? By which, I mean: if you are required to know and be familiar with a range of texts to meet your students' needs, or required to teach them as a set text, does your school pay for your ticket to go and see that play if a production is available? And if it doesn't, why not? Would our colleagues in English be asked to teach *The Handmaid's Tale* without being provided with a copy of it? Of course not. In fact, our subject goes beyond merely being familiar with the text in print. Yes, we need a physical copy of a play text if we are going to deliver it. (And on that topic, you should only be required to read that during the working hours for which you are paid.) But it is infinitely better for us, and for our students, if we have seen that play. Better yet, a range of plays. I'm not suggesting that you pop along and ask your headteacher for two tickets to *The Phantom of the Opera*, and maybe the train tickets and some money for a steak and a bottle of red beforehand. There's theatre-going for pleasure (which isn't how I would describe my visit to *The Phantom of the Opera*, but there you go) and there is theatre-going which supports our professional development and our students' learning. Now and again, one production can tick both of those boxes. Cheap tickets are often available. Many theatres, especially those subsidized with Arts Council funding, offer schemes for teachers which can include heavily discounted tickets. Finding the time to actually go to the theatre is one thing and should be our biggest hurdle. We should be able to expect professional support if we are willing to give up an evening (unpaid, of course) to go and see something which will help in the classroom. Or studio. Or portable cabin with a leaky roof. Some of you might read this and be thinking, 'No chance, you've not met my headteacher'. I probably haven't, but I think it's well worth going back to our guiding principles about thriving in the profession and what our expectations are. The bottom line is that if going to see a production of a particular play will directly support our teaching, then we should have every expectation that our schools will provide appropriate support to make sure this happens. And if we don't ask, then more fool us; we shouldn't sit waiting for schools to make us the offer.

If we find it difficult to get to the theatre, or afford it, or there isn't much on where you live, then there are other ways to keep in touch with the world of theatre-going. Most decent newspapers have still – just about – got theatre critics. The *Daily Mail* has one, too. Their reviews of current theatre productions can help us know what's on and steer us in the right direction if we are looking for something to bring into the classroom. Yes, theatre critics (many moons ago, I was one) are often derided for being negative, scornful and willing to trash a show. Whilst this is undeniably true in some cases, for the most part, theatre critics try and tell us if what they've seen is worth us paying hard-earned money for. Even if we can't get to see it, the rave reviews might prompt us to seek out a copy of the script itself. We can urge our students to get to see it if they are able. One of the biggest changes since I started teaching has been the shift in how theatres engage with the public. Whereas theatre reviews only ever used to appear in physical copies of actual newspapers, now it's routine to see theatre posters with quotes from bloggers, vloggers and a much broader range of critical viewpoints. This is emphatically a good thing, and we can also use these blogs and online reviews in our teaching. Have a look at what's out there – it's changing all the time – and sign up to some. Furthermore, if you can't get to the theatre, then it's easier than ever for the theatre to come to you. Sort of. I mentioned in Chapter 2 how useful NT Live (and other streaming theatre resources) can be in supporting our students. They can also be a great way for us to see high-quality live theatre, especially if we don't live within easy reach of London. Tickets to theatre broadcast into cinemas are, at the time of writing, roughly double what it costs to see the latest movie release. They are still far cheaper than most tickets to see the same production in person, with the associated costs of travel. Best of all, by virtue of the diligently choreographed camerawork, you get the 'best seat in the house'.

Then there is, of course, actually reading plays themselves, if the text is available. And it usually is. Yes, it's true that reading the play is not the same as experiencing the same play live in performance, but it is still another way for us to engage with contemporary work, stay relevant and keep up with what's going on in theatres. Scripts can be costly, but second-hand copies are frequently available online or from theatres directly. Some theatre companies have occasional sales of scripts from shows which they've produced. Whereas these boxes of texts are taking up valuable real estate in the offices of a theatre production company, they can be a relatively cheap way of adding to your play collection, whether this is at home or at work. By signing up to the mailing lists of theatres you'll be amongst the first to know if they ever decide to sell some of their texts. Charity shops can throw up the occasional gem, too. If I ever see a play text in a charity shop and think that there is even the vaguest chance that it might be appropriate to use with some of my students, then I buy it. When schools' departmental budgets are tight and the cost of buying play scripts isn't going to go down, we need to think creatively about how we might get them. All of us really should think about having a collection of plays. If you're reading this and worried that you don't have shelves groaning with hundreds of texts, then relax. It's more important to have a constantly growing repertoire of play texts which we might need to call into service as our students' needs demand. On top of which, we all of us have those plays we've never read or seen, just as we have all heard of films that we haven't watched and books that we haven't read. It's fine; we can't know everything. But if you know there's a gap in your knowledge of play texts, and you see an affordable opportunity to put that right, then do so.

If I could change one thing about the drama teaching profession as it currently stands it would be our collective reliance on the work of our colleagues and their own subject knowledge to help paper over the gaps in our own. I'll explain. When I started teaching, social media hadn't descended on our lives, but there were very active message boards as part of the TES forums online. Here, teachers would ask questions, share ideas, swap information and – there's absolutely nothing wrong with this – have a great big whinge. When I say they were very active, they were. But in the context of a world where people didn't have smartphones and couldn't be plugged into their online lives at all times. These forums are still going; they've mostly been monetized by people who are uploading their own schemes of work and selling them. And the good ones on there are very good indeed. It's fair to say, though, that the wealth of groups dedicated to drama teaching, and those which are then focused on specific exam boards at different levels, are active pretty much day and night. I can't see this changing any time soon either. Like any online area with only loose supervision and the ability for anyone to post at any time, what is posted online can be a real mixed bag. What usually makes up a significant portion of the traffic in drama teaching groups dedicated to social media is teachers asking if anyone might volunteer a lesson plan, a scheme of work or a suggestion of a text. It's certainly not unheard of for people asking for a lesson plan for something that they need to deliver the very next day. I think that we run the risk of devaluing our profession if we conduct ourselves like this online. I haven't done any forensic analysis or significant investigation, but I have seen examples of forums for teachers of other subjects, and the equivalent pleas for suggestions don't happen to anything like the same extent as they do in the drama world. There's an argument that because our subject has less structured definition from the outset, and there might well be more lone ranger departments, people need more help. This is only true to a point. It falls on each of us, as individuals, to have responsibility for our subject and the students we teach. If we, for instance, ask for suggestions for plays for our students, there is the inherent central flaw that whoever might make these suggestions doesn't know our students. If we use online forums to ask for suggestions, we might get some genuinely great ideas back. We might also get truly terrible ones, and it's going to take an awful lot of time to properly scrutinize the suggestions and tell the difference between good and bad. Don't get me wrong. I love being networked to other drama teachers. I am amazed at the hours that people put in, how hard they are willing to work and how much they evidently care for their students. But if we are going to be able to do our jobs well, then we need to go to the theatre. Or find a way to keep up to date with the profession. Or keep reading plays so that we look ever forwards rather than backwards. Next time you're thinking about posting on a social media forum – and someone once sent me a direct message about a play choice dilemma at 2 a.m. on New Year's Day – think whether the answers you might get back are going to help you to get to where you need to go. Might it be better to undertake a bit of research first, or to read a play? More time-consuming? Of course. But also definitely and emphatically better. And our students deserve us to be better.

Exploring cultural diversity

In 2007, the National Theatre staged an epic production of *A Matter of Life and Death*. This was directed by Emma Rice, on loan from running the celebrated Kneehigh Theatre, and an adaptation of a much-loved and popular film. Critical opinion seemed to be divided following press night. Whereas male theatre critics seemed to be fairly negative when reviewing the production, the play found much greater favour with female critics. As the theatre's serving artistic director (and champion of Emma Rice), Nicholas Hytner spotted this difference and launched an attack on the male critics of the play, describing them as 'dead white men'. There was uproar, albeit polite uproar amongst theatre critics and arts journalists. What Hytner had bravely done was point to the elephant in the room. Theatre and its history seem to be littered with and defined by (mostly) men. Most of them are dead. Most of them are white. And none of these men are women. At the moment, British theatre is in something of a transformative period and, frankly, it's way overdue. Compare a list of the most prominent and celebrated British playwrights working in 1980 to those working in 2000. Both lists are made up of virtually the same names. Michael Billington's excellent book *The 101 Greatest Plays* provides a short essay on each text, simultaneously demonstrating his astonishing breadth of knowledge and his years of service as a theatre critic. And yet, only six of these plays are written by women. To a point, this is unavoidable. Sweeping changes in the way that we live, at home and abroad, have meant that it is only recently that women have achieved the same prominence as men when it comes to playwriting and making theatre. Right now, we are poised at a moment where theatres are making more commitments to exploring cultural diversity than ever before. This isn't just a good idea for theatre; frankly, it's a good idea for all of us. Our subject is supposed to hold up a mirror to life and the world we live in, and part of our duty as drama teachers is surely to help our students explore and understand a world beyond their own lived experiences. As we think about how our teaching might meaningfully engage with contemporary work, it is certainly worth considering how we might implement an exploration of cultural diversity into what we do.

Firstly, what is cultural diversity? It's understanding and respecting the differences that are experienced by people living in different cultures. I've thrown in gender with my example above because, frankly, it would be mad not to, although it certainly doesn't stop there. We can think about exploring cultural diversity in terms of people of other nations, faiths, traditions, genders, sexualities. Here's the best part. It is so easy for our subject to do this in comparison with most other subjects. We are naturally poised to help students think about the world around them and to consider experiences other than their own. At the centre of our everyday classroom practice is a frequent need for people to put themselves in the shoes of others or pretend to be 'other'. Whilst we are doing this, it makes sense to think about opening up dialogues about cultural diversity. It's surprisingly easy to do so and has real educational value, within our subject and beyond it. For instance, the brilliant and popular musical *Everybody's Talking About Jamie* has really struck a chord with audiences everywhere. Sheffield Crucible's production moved to the West End in 2017 and shows no signs of going anywhere. Teachers love the show and so do their students. The show's tagline is '*The Hit Musical For Today*' and it's easy to see why. The show, focusing on an out-and-proud boy's dream of becoming a drag queen and wearing a dress to his Year 11 leavers' prom is as funny as it is moving. What Tom MacRae's script and Dan Gillespie-Sells' lyrics do is blast us with genuine wit and poignancy, whilst also tackling potentially thorny issues such as divergent gender identities, homophobic bullying (by kids and by adults) and what it feels like to live as a Muslim woman in contemporary Britain. The show touches on these things and – whether our students see it in person or read the script – can help us light the touchpaper to have group discussions which can help facilitate understanding of other cultures and identities. Bringing diverse cultural identities into our teaching doesn't even have to involve plays. At a department meeting recently, my colleagues and I were discussing the problem we have with our students who are very limited in terms of anything approaching organized movement, choreography or physical theatre. I teach in a single-sex school and the boys are bright, keen and happy to be tactile or play women if required to. The future Matthew Bourne dancers, though, they are not. We decided to step away from traditional drama work and now spend time teaching Year 7 students a complex haka dance when they start the school year. As well as improving the boys' movement, rhythm, coordination and collaborative skills, we are also introducing them to an ancient Maori tradition.

For those of us who do teach in single-sex schools, I think there is an increased level of responsibility for ensuring that our students aren't cocooned in their own bubble. A colleague of mine, who runs a book club for our students in partnership with a local girls' school, noticed that if the proposed book has a female protagonist or offers a 'female perspective on the world' (*The Color Purple* or *The Handmaid's Tale* would be good examples), then boys are less likely to read the book or attend the book club. I find that a bit depressing. I like to play a game with the students in my form where we compare our playlists on Spotify. Whilst they like to point out that my playlists are overly reliant on Kate Bush, David Bowie and Prince, I like to take the opportunity to point out that their playlists largely offer a musical perspective on the world which is the same as their own. I remind them that music by people who don't come from the same starting point as they do can offer us glimpses into other worlds and different ways of thinking. For all we might think that teenagers can be rebellious or anarchic (in their own teenage way), I am frequently reminded of how innately conservative they are. Most of them prefer to stick with the familiar and what they know. This is, to a point, understandable. None of us can change our fundamental starting point of what we are and who we are. But our lives are definitely enriched and our horizons can continue to be expanded by exploring and understanding how the artefacts, poems, stories, fables, words, pictures, sculptures, paintings and life experiences of others can make an impact on us.

For the sake of clarity, it's worth pointing out that there is nothing 'wrong' with being a dead white male, if we return to a criticism frequently levelled at theatre history. Nor can we change the past and some of the moments in theatre which seemed fine at the time but can make us wince now. I am as uneasy about the silencing of Kate in *The Taming of the Shrew* as I am about the physical transformation of Sandy at the end of the musical *Grease* and the message that this reinforces about fitting in and being accepted. And yet, both are products of different times and different cultures. Better, surely, to facilitate a discussion and debate about the more problematic points of some of our dramatic heritage than to ignore them, brush them aside or pretend that the tricky parts are absolutely fine. In so doing, we are more likely to help our students develop an understanding of the world around them and the world that went before them. Students who are willing to explore cultural diversities in this way are much more likely to make more diverse creative contributions and take risks in their own work, as well as having a better understanding of the nuances of some texts and performances. What's more, this isn't a fad or a phase. Theatre and performance, in a constant state of evolution and reinvention, are more diverse now than they have ever been. The work done by the formidable Act for Change project has started to have a real impact in terms of the representation of Black, Asian and minority ethnic actors on our stages. More women are running major theatres and arts organizations than ever before, alongside increasing commitments to stage more plays by women writers and with women directors. Those beloved plays by dead white men? They're still there and they aren't going anywhere. What British theatre is seeing at the moment is the beginning of an attempt to implement something of a balance so that our stages start to hold up a mirror to our nation and the wider world that we live in. Long may it continue. It can only be a good thing for us as teachers and for our students if we have an even greater and more diverse heritage of dramatic texts and performances to refer to. There aren't any losers in that scenario. And, if you're reading this and want to consign me to the corner marked 'lefty woke snowflake', then that's absolutely fine. It leads us nicely on to my final point in this chapter.

Drama: A political subject

A few years ago, one of my sixth form students developed something approaching a running joke in our lessons. I had taught him throughout his school career and he had developed into a keen drama student. His own views were very definitely to the right, politically, and he used to enjoy pointing out that every play that I had ever taught them and every theatre performance we had been to see was inherently left of centre. Where, he asked in earnest, were the right-wing plays? Why didn't we study plays which championed those on the right of the political spectrum? (He also used to struggle with the idea that a female actor could play Macbeth, but that's a conversation for another day.) It was very simple, I told him. There aren't many plays like that. Sure, there are plays which look at those on the political right: *The Resistible Rise of Arturo Ui*, *Top Girls*, *A Small Family Business*, to name a few. There are also plays which try to take an ambivalent look at both sides of the political coin. James Graham's superb play *This House* finds thrilling and highly charged drama in the political minutiae of the hung parliament of the 1970s (though I think Graham's own political leanings aren't too hard to spot). Likewise, Caryl Churchill's underrated (or, at least, underperformed) *Serious Money* shows the dizzy highs and frightening lows of the economic boom of Thatcherism in action. What I was trying to point out to my culturally conservative student was that theatre is in and of itself a political act. And that, politically speaking, playwrights and theatre makers tend to be left-wing. Theatre itself can be sneakily subversive in some ways but simultaneously manage to be doggedly predictable in its liberalist tendencies. Even my own GCSE students have worked out that a play like *Oh! What a Lovely War* is preaching to the converted. The Theatre Workshop play, steered by the indomitable Joan Littlewood, is very much a product of its time in terms of theatricality. Whilst its criticism of some of the decisions and behaviours of the top brass in the First World War might have once been seen by some as sacrilegious, it's unlikely that anyone has ever settled in to watch a performance of the play with a mindset which thinks that the Great War was actually pretty uplifting. In no way am I making a plea for more right-wing plays to be written and staged, but it can feel a bit like business as usual at times when we find a supposedly 'challenging' political play which reaffirms the status quo and trots out the consensus once again.

If we consider that plays and playwright are generally left-wing and created by those on the left of the political spectrum (and, arguably, *for* those on the same end of the playing field), then it's hardly surprising that the subject itself is, on an educational level, political too. Remember that discussion about drama's inclusion on the inaugural National Curriculum? Our subject was seen as being too inherently subversive and risked inspiring a generation of young rebels and anarchists, regardless of its literary virtues and its cultural heritage. As drama teachers, we can sometimes be eyed with suspicion by colleagues and parents. A few years ago, I used extracts from a television documentary about the Hillsborough disaster which was broadcast after the completion of the painstaking public inquest into what had happened and who was to blame. I thought this documentary was educationally sound and provided multiple perspectives, documentary and commentary on an important event which had occurred before my students had been born. On top of which, I found some of the testimony in the programme so moving that I had to watch it in several stages, pausing the film to blink back tears. A parent wrote to me, complaining that by not spending equal time in lessons 'promoting' the innocence of the police officers and their conduct on the day, I was attempting to politically brainwash their child. This was a tricky letter to reply to. Some years ago, I took my A level students to see a production of their set text *The Trojan Women* which had been relocated to the then-current Iraq War. Frankly, the opportunity to see a current set text in performance is one which should always be explored should it arise, and even though the production itself was a bit pedestrian, there were still some nice ideas which inspired students as they developed their own production concepts for the play. Several parents, however, wrote to my headteacher and complained that their children were being politicized. I'm not going to propose a solution to situations such as these, and they are thankfully rare. I mention these incidents to highlight that our subject has always been and will always be seen as inherently political. Whilst some outside of the subject looking in on it might see this as something to be wary of and proceed with caution, those of us who are teaching the subject could look to harness the power of its innately political nature.

I've been teaching the subject and involved with public examinations for long enough to know that the way that drama is dealt with in schools remains politically charged. Ofsted is supposed to be politically neutral and ensure that, regardless of the sitting government of the day and its political leanings, a decent standard of education is made available to all children through their compulsory schooling and beyond. The reality is very different. Too often it seems to be the case that our subject could be sidelined even further or – worst-case scenario – dropped altogether. When the educational reforms of 2014 were still at the discussion stage, some drama teachers wondered whether our subject would survive intact. In the end, of course, it wasn't dropped, but let's not forget that Performing Arts, as a discrete subject in its own right, was quietly discontinued. The prominence (or lack of prominence) of our subject in schools and the understanding of its real value can depend entirely on who's in charge and what their own beliefs are. I am infuriated when I hear the 'creative subjects' carelessly lumped together by a politician, or the assertion that subjects like ours are secondary in importance when compared to English, Maths or Science. At the moment, we have lost the battle for every student in the country to have a creative subject like ours as part of their curriculum profile. If that seems like a fanciful notion, it shouldn't do. As drama education specialists, we are often conditioned to think that our subject *shouldn't* stand alongside

Maths and English. Why shouldn't it? Answers on a postcard, please. Sometimes, frankly, we need to speak up a bit more and present the case for drama being *essential*. As part of the aforementioned reforms, when Ofqual was consulting with exam boards and theatre makers to help define the official subject content, they also reached out to teachers. Practising drama teachers could make their views heard as part of a survey at what was a critical juncture for the direction of the subject. Fewer than ten (ten!) teachers responded to this survey. Perhaps the survey wasn't publicized well enough. Maybe it kept falling to the bottom of our ever-growing 'to-do' piles of work and the deadline passed. Who knows? But it was perplexing to see drama teachers become very vocal about the direction that the subject was taking only *after* its core values had been defined and signed off by our governmental watchdog.

Not only can we use our subject to help students engage with the world around them, including its politics, whether these be party political or socially political, but we must also remember that ours is a subject that needs to be fought for. When I started my teaching career and the (New) Labour government was pumping money into schools and the educational sector, it seemed as though drama and the performing arts, which aren't always cheap to properly resource, were achieving real prominence and status, championed by those in charge. A decade of political and economic austerity later, and we have a subject which is still not thought to be important enough to exist as a discrete entity on our National Curriculum. The content of the subject at examination level, dictated centrally by Ofqual, is so restrictive that it's no surprise that all four exam boards' GCSE and A level specifications have so many similarities. And then there's us, the teachers, stuck in the middle. Delivering the subject at the chalkface and flying the flag for its inclusion. And yet. Drama teachers are, as a rule, passionate and dedicated to their subject. We frequently go above and beyond. There are extra hours which we give up willingly to try and make sure our students fulfil their true potential and do the best that they can. We can be booted out of our teaching spaces without warning (I was once asked by a senior manager in my last place of work to leave a drama studio with my A level group *in the middle of their dress rehearsal for their practical exam that evening* so he could chair a discussion about guide dogs), we sometimes have to beg, steal and borrow to get the funding together to make the school production go on, and the traffic on social media forums proves that drama teachers are thinking about their subject and their teaching pretty much round the clock. I think that the dedication of drama teachers is genuinely inspiring. But we must continue, as tiring as it can be, to state our case or fight our corner. We must respond to the urban myths and untruths which can sometimes surround our subject and shout about what it is that our subject *can* do. If it seems as though, throughout this book, I've placed an emphasis on you asking for things or standing up for what you need, then that's no coincidence at all. Sometimes we only get what we deserve. Which is not to say that we get what we need. If we don't have the correct budget or resources or teaching space to be able to deliver our subject, then we (and our students) are being set on a trajectory to disappointment and failure. This isn't good enough, and we need to speak up and state what we need. At the same time, we need to deliver the goods. Part of delivering the goods is staying abreast of what our subject does in terms of contemporary practice. Science and computer technology is constantly changing and so, to an extent, is the teaching of those subjects in our schools. Do our senior leadership teams know that drama is in constant evolution, too? If they don't, then we need to tell them. Given that we teach a subject which can inspire confidence in its students, maybe we need to think about how we can have a bit more confidence in the subject ourselves. The education of non-drama specialists about our subject starts with us and what we do. Next time there's a survey to be completed, fill it in. If you're not happy about the direction that drama is taking in schools, then get together with others who feel the same way and make your voices heard. We are the experts in our subject and we need to be the flag-waver, torch-carriers and standard-bearers for it. All at the same time, too.

6

The bits in between

No fixed route (sorry!)

Before I started my PGCE training, the people who ran the course suggested that I might want to go into some schools and see some drama teaching taking place, given that I hadn't set foot in a school since I was a student. This way, the tutors said, I could be sure that signing up for the course was the right thing to do. I was sent to Great Barr School in Birmingham. At the time it was the largest state secondary school in England, with around 2,500 pupils on its roll. It was truly comprehensive, and the intake of students was broad, drawing on a very ordinary, very English, very suburban housing estate which surrounded the school. During my time at Great Barr, I knew that I was about to sign up to the right course when I saw Kate Downie teaching. At that time, Kate was a graduate of the same PGCE course I was trying to get on to and running the school's very busy and very successful drama department. Kate ended up becoming my mentor when I was sent back to the school on a placement as part of my training and I was in awe of her. I had never seen (and have rarely seen since) a teacher who manages to make every student seem to want to do well in their lessons. Kate was truly inspirational. She's a friend now and we ended up on the same CPD training course recently, run by one of the exam boards. I was surprised to see her there; if I'm not sure about something, I'd ask Kate. So, what was she doing on this course? Simple. As we chatted, I realized that even the very best and most inspirational drama teachers need to shuffle the deck every now and again. If we reach the end of an academic year and think that everything has gone well, we might be inclined to rinse and repeat, trotting out the same content the following year. Whilst I fully understand the temptation to refer back to our former glories in the drama studio, we are also risking creating a different set of problems for ourselves. These problems can then become systematic both in our teaching and in our students' learning. Sadly, there is no singular, prescriptive and definitive one-size-fits-all route to an outstanding and creative curriculum and the successes that this brings. The best rule of thumb is not to have a fixed rule of thumb. Yes, your assessment framework can be rigorous and well structured. You can have a stockpile of play texts which might be able to be called into service. But it is very rarely the case, if at all, that the route of success for me and my Year 10 is going to look the same for you and your Year 10. We need to be willing to stop and reflect. Yes, this requires more work on our part, and is more demanding of us than for some of our colleagues in other subjects, but a willingness to engage in genuinely self-reflective practice is the key to preserving our sanity in the long run and guiding our students to success.

It is more likely that if we take risks (calculated risks, of course) and push ourselves we are able to meet the needs of our students and increase our own creativity at the same time. Along the way there might be some mistakes. This is fine. I repeat: this is fine. It obviously wouldn't be acceptable to make a mistake such as not entering a student for an exam or teaching the wrong set text, but if the benefits of being willing to adopt a 'no fixed approach' attitude mean that there is the occasional hiccup, then so be it. The best way to start is to look at each cohort, each class, each year group, each working group and think: what is the body of knowledge that we want to give to this *specific* group of students? That knowledge might come in the form of practical skills; it is the knowledge of what those skills are and how to successfully deploy them which is the important part. As a principle, it's better to plan and have several options available to us rather than working on a model of intervention and crisis management. This sort of approach perhaps won't suit everyone but does tend to yield the best results. I remember an NQT starting in my department a few years ago, proudly showing me his academic year planner, which had every single lesson mapped out for the entire academic year. This approach is, of course, commendable, but it's also fundamentally flawed. We need to have as much flexibility as possible in terms of the delivery of our subject, particularly in the years before students are working towards formal qualifications.

At the same time, our own training and development shouldn't stop at the moment we are handed our QTS certificate and told, '*Don't smile at them until Christmas*', and pushed towards our first steps of gainful employment in the profession. Our employers have a requirement to help nurture us as we make our way through the profession. Gaining valuable classroom experience is one thing, but we also need to experience proper and meaningful professional development. Schools have money which is allocated specifically for this. How they go about allocating that money is up to them, and it can vary enormously. In some schools, there is, sadly, a culture of turning down staff requests for training and development; a culture of, '*Can't it wait until next year?*' If you know that you're going to need help and support and need access to some of this funding, make sure you get your application in early. Be wary, also, of the schools who use dedicated time for continuing *your* professional development to focus on *their* statutory requirements. In busy schools where everyone is pushed for time, it's sad to see that statutory safeguarding needs (for example) can sometimes displace genuine opportunities for teachers to broaden their skills sets and reflect on their practice. I would suggest that it is even more of a rarity for drama teachers to have some sort of professional development which is subject-focused, or even for us to take part in more generalized pedagogical development where there is a consideration of our subject and our needs. If this isn't happening in your school, you are entirely within your rights to ask for it to be considered. I remember sitting through a two-day-long teacher training event in a school which was going to revolutionize my teaching and leave me full of inspiration. The reality was that it was deathly dull and left me full of tea and biscuits. At the end of the event, we were all given a copy of the speaker's book and told – by senior management – that we were now 'required' to demonstrate the speaker's methods in our lesson plans and schemes of work, as well as implement the techniques we had been shown in our teaching. Some of these techniques were fine, but in the entire two days of the speaker talking – which felt like a lifetime – there was not one single mention of drama, music, art or dance. It felt as though we were invisible if we were creative. We need, as I've said, to stand up and promote ourselves. We need to always have half a watchful eye on how we might raise and maintain our department's profile.

Raising your department's profile

Schools are busy. And not just every now and again. Schools are very busy absolutely all the time, and that's just the way it is. New initiatives come but they don't usually go, and there is often very little holistic thinking involved in terms of how the pressure can build on teachers and students. Most of these initiatives are individually quite manageable but can very quickly build to become a massive workload which leaves us crawling to the weekends and our paid annual leave. (Remember: they aren't school holidays, they are our paid annual leave.) How, then, do we make sure that our subject is seen and heard? It is harder than it has ever been to make an impact in busy schools which make sizeable demands on our time and energy. But we must. Our subject is starting with a handicap of sorts; it's not on the National Curriculum and, depending on the approach your school takes and whether they truly *value* drama and are willing to raise its profile and promote the subject, we could still find ourselves struggling for recognition. Fortunately, we do have some things which can work to our advantage and help us to raise the profile of our subject in our schools, and possibly beyond the gates as well. Our subject, in action, is great to photograph and film. We can show off what we do with relative ease. Letting people see what goes on in drama is actually quite easy for us to do, provided we plan in advance and make sure that we are well organized. Wise headteachers and senior leaders know that drama can be a great 'shop window' for their school as well as offering a clear demonstration of the standard of education in action. We need to tap into this and remember that part of our role is now – on top of everything else, and for better or worse – that of a salesman.

Performance is at the centre of our work, but it is logically sometimes thought of as the end product, and it's this end product which helps us most in raising our profile. (I can't imagine that watching hours of devised practical work in rehearsal would be thrilling for many people.) Performances require an audience; without an audience, it ceases to be a performance. There are so many opportunities to demonstrate the work that we do. This might be the school productions we direct. It could be the performances which make up practical exams at GCSE and A level. Maybe it's the work that the drama club does, or the showcases or curriculum work once a year for different year groups. With a bit of forward planning we can create performance events without having to generate much additional workload; the performances emerge as an organic part of the curriculum teaching. Make sure that you plan these as far as you can in advance. If your school uses a centralized calendar, get these performances booked on to it. Send an email to all the members of your senior management team at the start of the academic year so that they have all of these dates well in advance. We're all busy people with evening commitments and box sets to slump in front of, so we need to carefully schedule what we do as far in advance as possible. Performances will need promoting, too, to stand a fighting chance to be seen and heard above the everyday noise of school. Make sure that you send out posters, flyers, emails and letters to parents inviting them to come and see their child's practical work. Most parents love doing this; with a subject like ours where there might be an absence of exercise books, for example, it's great for us to show parents what it is that we do and what their child has been learning.

On a day-to-day basis, do everything you can to demystify the subject and what goes on in our teaching spaces. If you're comfortable with it, tell your colleagues that they can always consider the studio door to be open, even when it's closed. My current headteacher pops into lessons unannounced every now and again and will sit and watch groups at work or performing short pieces. This doesn't feel as though we are under scrutiny or that this is like a mini inspection. I'm pleased to have people see what's going on and it also serves to demonstrate that effective teaching and learning is taking place, even if there isn't an essay or a bursting exercise book at the end of it. I work in a busy department with five teachers currently and our communal office is connected to our practical teaching spaces. We can all see and hear what is going on in each other's lessons, day in and day out. We walk through each other's lessons all the time. Even if

I don't teach a student that one of my colleagues does, I will probably know a bit about them because we use our departmental meetings (and informal chats) to talk about our teaching, to share ideas and help each other out. It's a truly collaborative working environment, and if you are in a department like this or have the chance to build a department that works in this way, I would highly recommend it.

We can also help to raise the profile of our department by creating opportunities to demonstrate the work of the department beyond the walls of the school. When I taught vocational qualifications in sixth form colleges, we ran an annual project where students would form Theatre in Education companies and offer a performance of a play with a workshop for Key Stage 3 students to partner schools in the area. Unsurprisingly, schools jumped at the opportunity for this free resource. This is another example of a way in which a single task can tick off a bunch of requirements. Not only did the project fulfil their assignment brief as an assessment but it forged links with partner schools, raised the profile of the department (and the college) and gave students an insight into how the industry might work. Schools regularly invite other high schools or junior schools to watch public performances. It's best to make this a habit rather than an exception. Whilst it is undeniable that it will create some extra work – phone calls, risk assessments, the dreaded administrative burden – the long-term payoff makes it undoubtedly worth it in the end. Opportunities such as these make for impressive reading when Ofsted are looking to see how much impact we make on our students. In addition, it is a valuable opportunity to share best practice.

The idea of sharing best practice itself used to have a much higher profile in the day-to-day life of schools. I have a hunch, though, that it was used a bit like a hoop to jump through. To momentarily prove fleeting excellence rather than demonstrate that any such excellence was meaningfully embedded in the curriculum and its delivery. Now, it's more likely that sharing best practice will take place on a regular basis in schools. The sort of teaching that hasn't been designed to meet an inspector's set of criteria but rather to demonstrate genuine creativity and make a positive impact on our students. Talking to your colleagues, in your own subject and beyond it, is the best way to share good practice. And remember, if you don't have any in-house subject colleagues, then there are relatively easy ways to forge links. A few years ago, as we were implementing the new specifications at GCSE and A level and realizing that the amount of practical assessment work that we did had effectively doubled, my colleagues and I realized that we had less and less meaningful time to sit, discuss issues and share ideas. It was becoming harder and harder to celebrate what we did and share good practice. Somehow – I'm not exactly sure how we managed to sort this – we were allowed to have a departmental day off-site. A proper day of team building and sharing ideas. Did we want to go white-water rafting? No. What about one of those managerial away days where we would have to solve all sorts of outdoors-y problems using ingenuity and planks of wood? No thanks. All we wanted was a chance to sit down together, without the constant noise of emails, phone calls, knocking on the office door and bids for our time. That's what we did. We sat down together in an empty room, away from school, and filled sheets of flipchart paper with ideas. Loads and loads of them. Everyone pitched in. Then, we prioritized them and worked out what was immediate and what could wait. Some of them would require the go-ahead from senior management and some we could implement for ourselves. By the end of the day, we had what I suppose was something approaching a valid strategic plan for the department and how we were going to develop it. More importantly, though, was the fact that we had done the mental equivalent of cleaning out the kitchen cupboards and organizing all the stray parts for the food processor and chucking out all those glass ramekins from those mini desserts that we tend to horde. Everyone in the department had a stake in what we were going to do, and each person's contribution was clearly visible. That day revitalized us as teachers and as a department and was an important turning point. It was around six hours in a room with pens and paper. Nothing particularly fancy. I would urge you to do it. If you're in charge of a department, give it some serious consideration. It's tantamount to very cheap but highly effective professional development, plus biscuits.

Raising our subject's profile shouldn't be a battle and I am in no way advocating pitting our subject against another subject on the curriculum. We need to be as supportive and understanding of our colleagues' endeavours as we would wish them to be of our own. Where we might have to be prepared to shout a bit louder or act as a cheerleader for drama, though, is in situations where our leadership teams have no interest in the subject, or where they pretend to but don't do much in the way of demonstrating their interest or support. In a previous job role, when the headteacher phoned me after the day of the interviews and offered me the job, he flatly told me that he *'didn't like drama'*. Great, I thought, what a cracking start to my new role. I remember visiting a busy sixth form college in my work as an examiner and being escorted from reception to the drama studio by the deputy head. Making polite small talk as we negotiated the busy corridors, he told me, *'We're not really bothered about drama here, if I'm honest. As long as they don't fail, we just let them get on with it.'* I was momentarily speechless; there isn't really any decent response to a statement like that. Not only was it brazen, it showed a complete lack of respect for the subject and those who taught and studied it. I hope that you don't have senior leaders like that deputy head. But, as is so often the case, senior leaders are instrumental in dictating the tone of our schools, and this can sometimes leave us feeling that the deck isn't stacked in favour of drama. So, you can either accept the status quo, nod and allow the subject that you passionately believe in to be slowly eroded and downgraded through a tacit lack of support. Or, you can do what the most inspirational teachers do. Find ways to get noticed, to be heard, to stand out from the crowd. Do your bit to put the subject on the map and remember that our students deserve to have brilliant and – if possible – inspirational drama teaching.

Inspirational teachers

We hear the word inspirational (or inspiring) quite a lot, and probably more than we should. At its simplest, we can be inspired every single day, simply by being influenced or recognizing that something has prompted us to have an idea. When we start to think about people who are a genuine inspiration to us, especially in an educational setting, it's much harder to define. Your inspirational might well differ from my inspirational. And that's fine. It is certainly worth considering just how much impact a genuinely inspirational teacher can make on a student. Impact not just in terms of a school inspection framework but in terms of the sort of person who is long remembered, stands out from the crowd and inspires a dedication in a student; the sort of role model, if you will, who can influence and sometimes change the direction of a student's life, and for the better. I'm not sure that it's possible, and might even be seen as gross and cynical, to try and set out to be an inspirational teacher. In reality, some students are incredibly challenging to reach, never mind make an impact upon. On top of which, inspiration is usually deeply personal and certainly unique to the individual. And yet, we have a wealth of inspirational teachers around us as exemplified by plays, films and books. Maggie

Smith made the title role in *The Prime of Miss Jean Brodie* her own, but the play script by Jay Presson Allen set in stone the character of a most formidable schoolmistress. Dennis Kelly's witty book for the musical *Matilda* brought Roald Dahl's inspirational primary teacher Miss Honey to the stage, as well as the probably-shouldn't-be-an-inspiration-to-anyone Miss Trunchbull. And in cinema, Sidney Poitier, Robin Williams and Michelle Pfeiffer have created memorable educators who have inspired their challenging students in *To Sir, with Love*, *Dead Poets Society* and *Dangerous Minds* respectively. If we stand any chance of being an inspiration to any of our own students, we need to recognize what inspires us and how we can continue to feel personally inspired in our working lives.

Most of us will remember the teacher or teachers who inspired us when we were students ourselves. Teaching is a profession, but it's also a vocation. Without wanting to sound too like Maria in *The Sound of Music*, there is a passion for what we do which drives us and steers us through our time in the profession. From my own experience, I can remember being taught by some exceptional teachers during my time at school. Back then, of course, I certainly wouldn't have appreciated their classroom and behaviour management skills, their organization and rigour with assessment. What inspired me then, and still impresses me now, was their ability to be creative with the subject and how this creativity made me – and others – sit up, listen, pay attention and genuinely engage with the subject. My high school English teacher, John Morrison, taught us about how to understand poetry (which was baffling to me, a GCSE student being dragged through the syllabus) by using lyrics to Bob Dylan songs. Poetry was a world of unfamiliar words which didn't seem to make much sense. Pop songs, on the other hand, I liked. Many years later, I recognize that using songs to teach lyrics isn't an original invention. At the same time, several decades later, I can see that Mr Morrison was a teacher who was being genuinely creative with the curriculum and using one of *his* passions to help us navigate things that we didn't 'get' and would have been happy to turn away from. Because my English teacher was inspired, I was inspired in turn. Then, when it came to the 'strange' and unfamiliar verse and iambic pentameter of *Macbeth* I was more likely to sit up and listen, because this teacher would go out of their way to find ways to reach us. This is what the truly inspirational teachers do, I think. The best in our profession will find ways to meet all the compulsory requirements of what we do, and then find ways to go beyond this. I'm still impressed that my A level Theatre Studies teacher, Evette Harper, managed to get our class to learn, direct and perform a full production of Steven Berkoff's *Metamorphosis*. Not only that, but we had responsibility for set, costumes, make-up, promotion and music. She was in charge and steered the ship, but we were allowed to make decisions and had responsibility for getting the play on. What's most remarkable, looking back, is that this production wasn't part of our course and the text wasn't on the syllabus. Our teacher said that it was 'good for us' to have the experience and would give us something beyond the specification to talk about at future university admissions interviews. She was right, and she was also both brave and clever to give us this responsibility and let us explore this text and bring it to a performance standard at the same time as getting us through our demanding A level.

Having stated that we can't set out to 'be inspirational' (though I suppose it isn't a bad ambition to have) as teachers, what is certain is that we are only likely to inspire our own students if we, ourselves, feel inspired. Please don't throw the book across the room and think that I don't live in the real world. (I hate it when people tell teachers that they need a job 'in the real world'. I can scarcely think of other jobs which are any more truly real-world than teaching is.) Limping to the weekends and crawling to the end of term tends to be the norm for all of us, and I'm sure that the red tape and multiple demands on us now are far greater than those on my A level drama teacher some twenty years ago. The trick is to work out what things inspire you, or make your pulse race a little bit faster, and make a note of them. Keep a list, or a folder, or a shelf. But do keep track of these things. It could be *anything*, even things that don't appear to be directly connected to the subject. I met a science teacher once who kept the wheel of their bike above the desk in their teaching space. The teacher had been knocked off their bike by an errant lorry and had very nearly died. He told me that the bike wheel was his daily reminder of how very lucky he was to still be alive. That was all the inspiration he needed. For those of us who might not choose to keep a visible keepsake of any brushes with death we may have had, we can still keep a reminder of the little things which keep us going. Without wanting to come across as too ethereal and floaty, it is these things which can help remind us about why we do what we do. With all the inherent stresses that come with the profession, it can be hard, sometimes, to keep sight of the best parts. When I remember to practise what I am preaching here, I remind myself of how lucky I am to use my degree subject knowledge every day, and that the best parts of being a teacher simply can't be replicated and don't exist in other professions. Try, then, to keep sight of what it is that drives you and gets you fired up. If at all possible, keep a physical reminder of this. I have devoted playlists to songs which have a particular significance to me. Above my desk is a postcard of the barn near the Cornish cliffs where Kneehigh Theatre rehearse and create their shows, bonding as a company along the way. In moments where I'm feeling that my teaching is at risk of becoming boring or pedestrian (those afternoon lessons when it's wet and dark outside and the end of term seems a million miles away), I look at the barn and remember that such an unlikely wooden building has been a breeding ground for some of the most popular and energized theatre of recent times, which has gone on to make an impact with audiences around the world. Next to this photo sits a photo of a retired colleague whose patience and kindness with students serve as a reminder to try and not sigh when one of them knocks on the door. These are tokens; emblems, if you like. Not for a moment would I suggest that these things could sustain me through a year at work, but if I have reminders of why I love what I do, they help me to cut through all the admin and paperwork and focus on drama teaching at its best. In so doing, with a bit of luck, and with the wind behind us, if we are focused on what we do, we stand every chance of being an inspiration to our students, who will remember us – and what we did – for many years to come.

The coat or the hanger

Ultimately, I suppose that if there's any way to conclude a book on what I have learned through fifteen years of teaching, working with colleagues in schools and toiling in public examinations, the process comes full circle. The question that I was posed as a young-ish, keen trainee PGCE student is still as relevant and pertinent as ever. And I still don't have a solution for it. To recap: is drama the coat or is it the coat hanger? Is it the subject in its own right with performance as the end product (the coat, all new and clean and shiny, ready to be looked at and praised by the public) or is it a medium through which we can deliver content (the coat hanger, sturdy and ready to be dressed with something eye-catching, all the time supporting the weight of the coat)? The 'logical' and well-considered response is that it isn't one thing *or* the other and that it is a fascinating and complex mixture of both. Our subject can't always be so easily separated into such binary 'units', and there's an argument that it makes even less sense and has even less value if we try to do this. But that robs the question of its real purpose and any sense of fun. We need to keep asking ourselves questions such as these so that we stay engaged with what we do. All of us who have chosen to teach drama have made a decision to never be millionaires. And in return we are privileged to have the opportunity to be involved with educating the next generation. Not only that, we can be constantly engaged and energized by an ever-changing art form and pass on our love for our subject to those that we teach. None of us are likely to have become drama teachers without, somewhere along the way, encountering a brilliant and inspirational drama teacher ourselves. This might be a school drama teacher but could have been a weekend drama club coach or a skilled amateur dramatist. The point is that we are still here, as drama teachers, relegated from the so-called respectability of the National Curriculum, making sure that our voices are heard and that our subject is essential and has a chance of surviving and – ideally – thriving.

If we don't keep asking ourselves questions about the coat and the hanger, or any equivalent metaphor that you might choose to land on, then we run the risk of becoming stale. I hope that, as retirement starts to loom on the horizon one day (though with the ever-changing pension age creeping up all the time, there's every likelihood that the government will set my retirement age at around 120), I don't decide that the last few years in the profession don't matter as much and consequently allow my teaching to become stale. Students deserve us at our best. In turn, if we are going to stand a chance of being the best we can be, we need to have the appropriate level of guidance and support from our schools and senior colleagues. Some days I am convinced that it's all about the coat; the performance that students create is the one which they will remember, it's the one they can write about and it unites us in the room and we are drawn into the story unfolding. We are neuro-linguistically programmed to be drawn to stories, to narrative, so – of course! – this is the best way to capture our attention and get us to engage. It's the coat, of course. And, then, on other days, I think it's all about the hanger. How could it not .be? Only by getting involved in the research around the subject, by digging into the topic and by asking those searching questions can we stand a chance at improving and becoming better at what we do. Furthermore, we stand more of a chance of learning more about a wider range of topics and subjects. So how could it be anything other than the hanger? And then there are the moments when I will have these conflicting thoughts in the same day, or even in the same lesson. Find out the question that is going to keep you going and pin it above your desk at work.

Drama isn't an easy subject to teach, just as it isn't an easy or soft option to study. Whilst I understand the rationale behind the government's decision to lure science and maths graduates into the teaching profession with juicy cash incentives, it can also look pretty insulting to the likes of us. A two-tier system has been created whereby the current government feels that graduates in science and maths are somehow worth more than we are, in terms of salary. This is absolute nonsense, of course. Drama teachers have to create their own framework beyond the meagre three mentions of our subject which appear within the National Curriculum in English. We have to deliver complex theory through practice. We are writers, directors, counsellors, academics, leaders and, on our best days, we are keeping arts visible in schools as part of an education system which doesn't insist that every child has a right to a compulsory education in a creative subject. I hope that this changes and that, one day, we are led by politicians and influential leaders who understand that the value of something is measured in much more than mere fiscal terms, and that our subject has been at the forefront of civilization for thousands of years.

We mustn't settle for not being properly supported in our schools and we must not be ignored or short-changed by our senior leadership teams. And we need to get better at asking for what we need and ensuring that we get it. We need to go to the theatre, and read plays and talk to and network with our subject colleagues, in our own schools and beyond. It has never been easier to do so. There are national organizations which exist to unite us as subject specialists and promote what we do. Think about joining one and buying into a subject which can change lives and and mean you're surrounded by like-minded souls. Whether you think it's the coat or you're convinced it's the hanger, our subject remains brilliant and complex, academic and fun, demanding and hugely enjoyable. A few years ago, when I was writing one of the new specifications for GCSE Drama, I was leading a group discussion with a panel of teachers. They were all very keen to have their say about what direction these new specifications should take. At the same time, other subjects were being reformed and the media (or the part of the media which keeps a beady eye on the goings-on in education) was full of academics and politicians talking about STEM subjects and how our students needed to be able to stand shoulder to shoulder with students from the Far East in a competitive global employment market. One of the teachers banged her pen on the desk, threw her head back and let out a throaty howl of protest. It was designed to have a comic effect, and it certainly did, startling the room of drama teachers, each one with a jaunty scarf and a copy of a broadsheet newspaper. '*What they don't get,*' she said, once she'd finished her howl of frustration, and referring to those who are in charge of us and our profession, '*is that we are* people.' She went on. Explaining that we aren't numbers or symbols or a currency value, or a carbon-based unit attached to a computer processor. We are, people, humans, with emotions, peering out at the world around us and trying to make sense of it. She won a round of applause. She was right. How, without drama, would we even begin to make sense of the world around us? And that's another question, much like the one about the coat and the hanger, for which I don't have an answer.

Afterword: Finally and most importantly – you

Before I focus on the most important part of all of this, which is you, I'm going to explain a little bit about me.

I never had any plans to be a drama teacher. It just sort of happened. When I left university, having studied drama for three years and having been surrounded by (and lived with) wannabe actors, writers and directors, I confidently announced that I wanted nothing more to do with drama. Sure, I might go to the theatre or the cinema every now and again, but as a subject? I was done with it. It's not that my degree and time at university were bad. Far from it; I had a great time, racked up loads of debt and learned a lot about drama and theatre. I think that I had reached something of a saturation point with the subject. After awarding myself the summer holidays 'off' – those final exams and parties afterwards can *really* take it out of you – I started looking for a job. Unlike my friends, I wasn't trying to get into drama school or secure funding to be a trainee assistant director. No, I meant a proper job, a *real* job, in the real world. I'd had temporary holiday jobs in flash offices in the holidays and knew that's where my future surely lay. Nothing to do with drama, thank you very much. Somehow, and after a series of demanding interviews, I was appointed with the lofty title of Recruitment Executive. If the idea of working as an IT recruitment consultant in a Birmingham office block, just after the dot-com bubble burst, doesn't sound especially exciting, then let me assure you: it was much worse than that. I don't wish to denigrate any profession which isn't teaching, but I had assumed that all the temporary jobs I'd done whilst at university were rubbish because they were temporary. Not so; they were rubbish because they were absolutely not the job for me. Within a week, I realized that it was my pesky drama skills which had helped me talk my way into this role. I didn't know the first thing about recruitment or computers, but very soon realized that it was my confidence and communication skills which had gotten me into this fine mess. Recruitment work wasn't for me. At this stage, it never occurred to me to fall back on my degree specialism. After two months in the role, and evidently taking no amount of enjoyment from it (*'Why don't you ring the office sales bell, Matthew, and celebrate your win for the team?'*), I resigned. It was Christmas time. I was broke. I walked through the streets of Birmingham carrying a cardboard box with everything from my desk, and it started to rain. Great. I had no idea what to do next.

In the New Year, a friend of mine who was a mostly-out-of-work actor said that he was – to his surprise – quite enjoying his work as a classroom assistant in a high school. Much more satisfying than bar work or office work, and with the bonus of being finished by three o'clock. I promptly joined a teaching supply agency and waited for the phone to ring. I only had to wait for three days. The recruitment consultant phoned me on a Sunday evening and said she was *desperate*. She needed a drama teacher for the next day to go to a school on the other side of the city and deliver a lesson, and please would I do it? I spluttered. I don't have a teaching qualification, I'm twenty-one, I've not been in a classroom since I was at school myself, I protested. No need to worry, she said. Let her get on with telling the school that I was a qualified teacher (and look no further should you ever doubt the ethics of the recruitment profession) and the school would provide the lesson plans and schemes of work for me. Job done. And, what's more, it would be paid double the day's rate for being a classroom assistant. Flat broke and full of January gloom, I agreed.

The school was notionally a specialist performing arts college, but what that really meant was a building with fantastic spaces for delivering drama and dance lessons, and an entirely ineffectual senior management team, a demoralized staff and some seriously challenging students. My first day was a baptism of fire and I was clearly both clueless and out of my depth. It felt like every profession I was trying my hand at was the wrong one. But there was something that flickered to life inside me, the feeling of genuinely understanding drama and theatre, which I'd gained from my degree. To cut a long story short, I ended up working at this school for the remainder of the academic year. I made the dodgy recruitment consultant 'fess up and tell the Head of Department that I was unqualified and would need some proper support; the departmental staff were amazingly kind and patient with me. In those two terms, I learned all of the rookie mistakes that trainee teachers make, mainly by doing them unintentionally and then wondering why chaos reigned in the drama studio as well as working out how best to correct my mistakes. Within a week, about the same length of time that it had taken for me to know that recruitment wasn't the job for me, I sort of fell in love with drama teaching. I joined the school in January and was the students' sixth (sixth!) drama teacher since the start of the academic year in September. No one had stayed. Slowly, over time, once the kids began to realize that I wasn't going anywhere, they grew to trust me. Some of them even started to enjoy their lessons. I remember standing at the back of the drama studio with the proper drama teachers as the students performed their devised pieces at GCSE for the visiting examiner and felt a mixture of pride, nerves and satisfaction at having made a difference. Those feelings are the exact same ones I have when I watch my own students' exam performance work now, nearly two decades later.

I hope that this book has been useful, and I wish someone else had written it two decades ago when I was making my first steps in the drama teaching profession. Not that I think, for a minute, that this book is only useful to newcomers to the profession. I've tried to put forward and explain everything that I've learned along the way through being a classroom teacher as well as the other jobs I've had. It's important to stress: I never had a plan. I still don't. I have been incredibly fortunate to have been mentored by and to have taught alongside some genuinely inspirational professionals. The drama teaching community itself constantly amazes me with the amount of time and dedication its members willingly devote to the subject and those who we teach. Meeting hundreds of drama teachers at courses and events I've run has been a complete joy. And it's always reaffirmed my view that we are all in this together. At every course or event that I've ever run, I have always walked away having learned something new about my subject, or the delivery of my subject. We are each other's best resource. But, sometimes, it's hard to feel brilliant, inspirational or strong. I suspect that many of us start each new academic year full of goodwill and pledges to ourselves about the sort of teacher that we will be, and what we want to do. And by October half-term, many of us might feel that we have fallen far short of that. Yet, whenever I work with teachers in other schools, that's not what I see. What I see is the blood, sweat and tears of brilliant teachers trying their best and wanting our students to do the very best that they can.

The teaching profession has become more and more demanding since I started, and the delivery of our subject hasn't got any easier either. In that respect, it can be easy to feel a failure, but I promise you that you're not. The amount of paperwork to complete a theatre visit, for example, is extraordinary. A decade ago, it was much simpler. Our subject is also physically demanding. We don't often teach whilst sitting at a desk. We can be on our feet an awful lot and have to shout above the noise of groups of students working excitedly. And loudly. Let us never underestimate that our jobs require immense specialist skill and can also really take it out of us. It's no secret, of course, that many teachers don't last very long in the profession once they have completed their initial teacher training. I remember after the financial crash of 2008, many white-collar workers facing redundancy decided that they would retrain as teachers. Most of them didn't last long in the profession. The recruitment of teachers has its peaks and troughs, and is often dictated by the political agenda of the day. When I trained to be a teacher, the government threw lots of attractive incentives our way. That doesn't happen now, and tuition fees are much higher than they were. Today, if you want to be a drama teacher, you have to *really* want to be a drama teacher.

Whether you are a newly qualified teacher, or you're in training, or you've been in the profession for years, let me stress the importance of being kind to yourself. Amongst the many changes that I've seen since I've started teaching has been a shift in the way that we talk about mental health and well-being. The focus is still on our students, and if we hear of an 'epidemic' in terms of a crisis in young people's mental health, then we shouldn't be surprised. People are more and more willing to talk about how they feel and how they are coping. Or not coping. I want to see a real shift in how we start to look after the mental health and well-being of teachers. And especially drama teachers. All the advice and suggestions in this book are pretty well redundant if you aren't in a position where you can function properly and cope. Let me stress again: drama teaching can be demanding and exhausting. We have to deal with emotions and sensitive subject areas on a regular basis, and this can affect our own mental health and well-being. There is an increased emphasis on this area, with more people being trained in schools as mental health first-aiders. But is there enough support for teachers, who are the engine room of the profession? I am not convinced that there is, and we need to be as supportive of one another and as protective of our subject area as we are able to be.

Start with you. The notion of self-care isn't especially new, but it's less likely to be scoffed at than it was in the past. You can only deliver the goods in the classroom (or studio, or leaking portable cabin), you can only stand a chance at being brilliant and inspirational, if you are feeling healthy and happy. Years ago, mental health was mostly mumbled about, even in schools, with people suggesting that anyone feeling anxious or depressed needed to 'pull themselves together'. I sincerely hope that those days are behind us and we are slowly shifting into territory where we drama teachers can ask for help when we need it and know that our senior leadership teams and schools are willing to provide it. It's absolutely the case that we need to support our students in terms of their mental health and well-being. But we also need to make sure that we are supportive of each other as a community of subject professionals, and that we also take the time to be kind to ourselves. It's a two-way street. We need to be brilliant teachers (I'm trying not to describe us as outstanding teachers, for all of the obvious connotations which that word brings with it) who can be ambassadors for our subject and pass it on to the next generation of students and teachers. Teachers who are willing to say, yes, drama is *essential*. This can only happen if our schools are supporting us. Too many schools and senior leadership teams expect their drama teachers to work miracles with inappropriate funding and a lack of resources. The expectation of our workloads and how we might spend our free time can also be insulting if our managers don't provide enough support. We are only paid to complete the job during our working hours. Your workload should be commensurate with the amount of time that you are paid for. If your school isn't providing appropriate support and won't help you, remember that you are paid for your time. Any work that you do outside of working hours is as a result of your goodwill. We all of us want to do the best for our students, but we also mustn't let ineffective senior leadership teams take advantage of our goodwill and add to our stress levels unnecessarily. That stress is likely to have a direct impact on your physical and mental health. We need our schools to support us if they want to get the best out of us. It's as simple as that.

I have met drama teachers who are frazzled and at the end of their tether because they are terrified about their students' results, or fret that they are underperforming. In the majority of cases, when I meet someone who is pulling their hair out and close to tears, it is usually more about them lacking confidence. Oh, the irony. For a subject in which we deal in communication, in standing up in front of strangers and pretending to be someone else and saying made-up words, in making our students speak louder and draw attention themselves, we aren't always very good at having confidence in our own abilities. We expect our students to show confidence (the word confident, or variants of it, appears in most exam boards' mark schemes at some stage) but don't always believe in ourselves. Let's make a pact to stop that. If you've read this far, then it's evident that you care about drama and that you want to be a brilliant drama teacher. I want us – all of us – to thrive, not just survive, in the profession. But also, I want all of us to excel and to inspire and to communicate the sometimes undefinable magic of our precious and brilliant subject to those in our classrooms. Let's make a pact to look after ourselves. To be kind to one another, in person and online. Let's do all that we can to keep ourselves up to date and informed about the world of drama teaching and the world of theatre-going. Let's be sure to read some plays and get to the theatre. Let's be sure to rip out that brilliant newspaper article when we see it, or to scribble down the name of that podcast which might be perfect for that Year 9 lesson next week. Let's not be afraid to ask for help. Absolutely all of us get things wrong from time to time. If we make a mistake, let's be big enough to admit it, even if that means telling a group of students that we got something wrong. Let's agree to look forwards and not backwards. There's nothing wrong with *Blue Remembered Hills*, but other plays are available. Lots of them. Let's be willing to help each other out and share ideas, but not expect our drama colleagues online to do our lesson and resource planning for us or recommend plays for our students who they probably don't know. Let's be willing to show off our subject and be proud of all that it does as part of a school community. Our subject can be the shop window for a school, but it can also nurture genuinely collaborative and creative experiences which bring people together. Let's remember to get on top of our paperwork as often as we can and to empty our inboxes. Is it essential to have your school email address connected to your phone? I'd argue that it isn't and that we all need room to breathe and some headspace when we are away from work. Let's not be frightened of exam boards and remind ourselves that they can provide help and support and resources which can be invaluable in our teaching. Rather than seeing 'the board' as a faceless Borg-like enemy, let's remember that exam boards need our business and want us to continue to deliver their specification. Let's do all that we can to design an exciting and rigorous creative curriculum which serves our students up to and through their GCSE and A level years. At the same time, let's not lapse into repeating the same content year after year, and be willing to step back and reflect on what we've done and make changes where necessary. Each of us is different and, whilst they will share similarities, our students are different too.

Let's aim to be brilliant and inspirational and – okay, if you want – outstanding. But at the end of the day, we drama teachers are only human, teaching other younger humans about people and feelings and the way that the world works. It's absolutely enough to aim to survive in the profession. But if we aim to be our best, our very best, and we can help our students connect with our subject and find their passion too, then that's a job well done. When we do this, we are thriving. Drama can save lives. That's no exaggeration. It can equip you with the skills to blag your way into a job in IT recruitment. It can teach you how to make a box model. You can learn how to play *Hedda Gabler*. And you can learn about who you are and your own place in the world. What other subject can do that? Drama is essential in all our lives. It's a truly brilliant subject and it's a real privilege to be able to teach it.

Let's get to it.

Acknowledgements

No one is more surprised than me that I've actually finished the book, and this means that I can stop complaining about not having finished it. I'm really grateful to a fair few people for their support, advice, encouragement and brilliance along the way.

To Anna Brewer, for taking a chance on me and steering me through the project with unending patience. The entire team at Bloomsbury, as well. Especially Meredith Benson, Dom O'Hanlon and fellow series editors Sara E. Freeman, Chris Megson and Jenny Stevens.

Maggie Gale, for all her wisdom and advice on how to actually sit down and write a book.

I'm so lucky to have been taught how to teach by the inspirational Simon Spencer at Birmingham City University (BCU), as well as learning alongside the hilarious Julia Watkins.

The reason I wanted to be a drama teacher in the first place is because of Kate Downie, and her values and attitude in the classroom are what got me started. I've also taught alongside amazing subject colleagues along the way: Lucy Huntbach, Charlotte Tildesley, Martin Travers, Clare Howdon, Lucy Atkinson, Ted Moore and Louise Power.

My current department at Manchester Grammar School (MGS) really is the very best and I love working alongside my department colleagues. Sean Abbs, Sarah Bell, Kath Hellier, Jackie Sherratt, Kim Tetley – thank you. You're ace.

And to Martin Boulton, Michal Lowe, Neil Smith and Paul Thompson, also of MGS, who were flexible enough in allowing the department to work for exam boards and gain such valuable insight into the subject.

A few years ago, when things were tough, a select few drama teachers really were very kind to me. Helen Avouris, Jill Haves, Aisha Mian – thank you so much.

I'm also so grateful to have worked with and learned from Annmarie Conway ('You and your jazz haircut'), Alex Cooper, Amanda Fitzsimons, Nicky Jessop, Sally Marchant (friend, mentor, all-round joy) and Adele Waites (who won't have read this far down the page). You are all outstanding at what you do.

To all my students, past and present; thanks for unknowingly providing all of the anecdotal filling for this book.

Billie Andrews – I'm incredibly lucky to have you in my life. Thanks for helping me keep my head above water, and for always asking how many words I'd written.

And to my friends who now don't have to hear me complaining about how I can't play out because I have to write the book, but have been mega supportive and pretended to be interested: Fiona Button, Karen Duffy, Lissy Gunning, Paul Gunning, Jenefer Hughes, Gareth Joyner, Matt O'Neill, Jessica Nichols, Sarah Power, Jess Ransom, Carl Thornley, Ben Turner. You were all there when things got tough. Thank you.

And, finally, to those special few who really do have the patience of saints: Aaron Cornish, Kelly Cullen, David Leith, Andrew Hollingworth and Jack Tattersall. I did it. I wrote a book.

Index